Reach Your

LIBRA

Teresa Moorey

Dedication

For my son, Adam, for my Mother, and for Lyn

ISBN 0 340 69715 6

First published 1998
Impression number 10   9   8   7   6   5   4   3   2   1
Year   2002   2001   2000   1999   1998

Typeset by Transet Limited, Coventry, England.
Printed in Great Britain for Hodder & Stoughton Educational, a division of
Hodder Headline plc, 338 Euston Road, London NW1 3BH by Cox & Wyman,
Reading, Berkshire.

Contents

Introduction

A PERSPECTIVE OF ASTROLOGY

Interest in the mystery and significance of the heavens is perhaps as old as humanity. If we can cast our imaginations back, to a time when there were no street lamps, televisions or even books, if we can picture how it must have been to have nothing to do through the deep nights of winter other than to sit and weave stories by the fire at the cave mouth, then we can come close to sensing how important the great dome of stars must have seemed in ancient times.

We are prone to believe that we are wiser today, having progressed beyond old superstitions. We know that all stars are like our Sun – giant nuclear reactors. We know that the planets are lumps of rock reflecting sunlight, they are not gods or demons. But how wise are we in truth? Our growing accumulation of facts brings us no closer to discovering the real meaning behind life. It may well be that our cave-dwelling ancestors knew better than us the meaning of holism. The study of astrology may be part of a journey towards a more holistic perception, taking us, as it does, through the fertile, and often uncharted realms of our own personality.

Until the seventeenth century astrology (which searches for the meaning of heavenly patterns) and astronomy (which seeks to clarify facts about the skies) were one, and it was the search for meanings, not facts that inspired the earliest investigations. Lunar phases have been found carved on bone and stone figures from as early as 15,000BCE (Before Common Era). Astrology then evolved through the civilisations of Mesopotamia and Greece, among others. Through the 'dark ages' much astrological lore was preserved in Islamic countries, but in the fifteenth century astrology grew in popularity in the West. Queen Elizabeth I had her own personal astrologer, John Dee, and such fathers of modern astronomy as Kepler and Galileo served as court astrologers in Europe.

Astrology was taught at the University of Salamanca until 1776. What is rarely appreciated is that some of our greatest scientists, notably Newton and even Einstein, were led to their discoveries by intuition. Newton was a true mystic, and it was the search for meaning – the same motivation that inspired the Palaeolithic observer – that gave rise to some of our most brilliant advances. Indeed Newton is widely believed to have been an astrologer. The astronomer Halley, who discovered the famous comet, is reported to have criticised Newton for this, whereupon Sir Isaac replied 'I have studied it Sir, you have not!'

During the twentieth century astrology enjoyed a revival, and in 1948 The Faculty of Astrological Studies was founded, offering tuition of high quality and an examination system. The great psychologist Carl Jung was a supporter of astrology, and his work has expanded ideas about the mythic connections of the birth chart. Astrology is still eyed askance by many people, and there is no doubt that there is little purely scientific corroboration for astrology – an exception to this is the exhaustive statistical work undertaken by the Gauquelins. Michel Gauquelin was a French statistician whose research shows undeniable connection between professional prominence and the position of planets at birth. Now that the concept of a mechanical universe is being superseded, there is a greater chance that astrology and astronomy will reunite.

Anyone who consults a good astrologer comes away deeply impressed by the insight of the birth chart. Often it is possible to see very deeply into the personality and to be able to throw light on current dilemmas.

It is noteworthy that even the most sceptical of people tend to know their Sun sign and the characteristics associated with it.

■ WHAT IS A BIRTH CHART?

Your birth chart is a map of the heavens drawn up for the time, date and place of your birth. An astrologer will prefer you to be as accurate as you can about the time of day, for that affects the sign rising

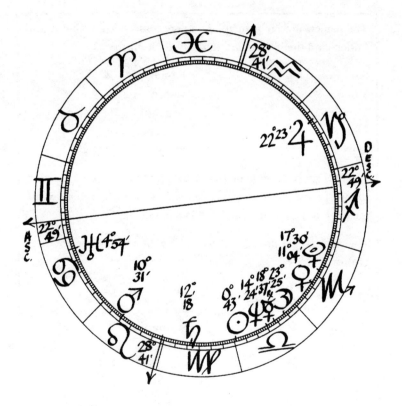

The birth chart of Bruce Springsteen
It can be seen that the singer has Sun ☉, Moon ☽, Mercury ☿ and Neptune ♆ in Libra, so intensifying charm and artistic abilities.

on the eastern horizon. This 'rising sign' is very important to your personality. However, if you do not know your birth time a chart can still be compiled for you. There will be some details missing, but useful interpretations may still be made. It is far better for the astrologer to know that your birth time is in question than to operate from a position of false certainty. The birth chart for Bruce Springsteen (page 3) is a simplified chart. Additional factors would be entered on the chart and considered by an astrologer, such as angles (aspects) between the planets, and the houses.

The **planets** are life principles, energy centres. To enable you to understand the birth chart, here are their glyphs:

Sun	☉	Jupiter	♃
Moon	☽	Saturn	♄
Mercury	☿	Uranus	♅
Venus	♀	Neptune	♆
Mars	♂	Pluto	♇ (♇)

Rising Sign or **Ascendant** (**ASC**) is the way we have of meeting the world, our outward persona. **Midheaven** (**MC**) refers to our image, aspirations, how we like to be seen.

The **signs** are modes of expression, ways of being. Here are their glyphs:

Aries	♈	Libra	♎
Taurus	♉	Scorpio	♏
Gemini	♊	Sagittarius	♐
Cancer	♋	Capricorn	♑
Leo	♌	Aquarius	♒
Virgo	♍	Pisces	♓

Using knowledge of the glyphs you can see that the Sun is in Gemini in our example birth chart (page 3).

The birth chart shows each of the planets and the Moon in the astrological signs, and can be thought of as an 'energy map' of the different forces operating within the psyche. Thus the Sun sign (often called 'birth sign' or 'star sign') refers only to the position of the Sun. If the planets are in very different signs from the Sun sign, the interpretation will be greatly modified. Thus, if a person has Sun in Leo yet is somewhat introverted or quiet, this may be because the Moon was in reserved Capricorn when that person was born. Nonetheless, the Sun represents the light of consciousness, the integrating force, and most people recognise that they are typical of their Sun sign, although in some people it will be more noticeable than in others. The planets Mercury and Venus are very close to the Sun and often occupy the same sign, so intensifying the Sun-sign influence.

This book is written about your Sun sign, because the Sun sign serves as an accessible starting point for those wishing to learn about themselves through astrology. However, do not let your interest stop there. If you find anything helpful in comments and advice stemming from Sun sign alone, you will find your true birth chart even more revealing. The address of the Faculty of Astrological Studies appears in 'Further Reading and Resources' at the back of this book, and it is a good idea to approach them for a list of trained astrologers who can help you. Moon *phase* at birth (as distinct from Moon sign) is also very important. *The Moon and You for Beginners* (see 'Further Reading') explains this fascinating area clearly, and provides a simple chart for you to look up your Moon phase, and learn what this means for your personality.

■ HOW DOES ASTROLOGY WORK?

We cannot explain astrology by the usual methods of cause and effect. In fact, there are many things we cannot explain. No one can define exactly what life is. We do not know exactly what electricity is, but we know how to use it. Few of us have any idea how a television set works, but we know how to turn it on. Although we are not able to explain astrology we are still able to use it, as any capable astrologer will demonstrate.

Jung discovered something called 'synchronicity'. This he defined as 'an acausal connecting principle'. Simply, this means that some events have a meaningful connection *other than cause and effect.* The planets do not cause us to do things, but their movements are synchronistic with our lives. The old dictum 'as above, so below' applies here. It is a mystery. We can't explain it, but that doesn't mean we should refuse to believe in it. A little boy on a visit to the circus saw an elephant for the first time and said 'There's no such thing'. We may laugh at the little boy, but how many of us respond to things we do not understand in this way?

The planetary positions in your birth chart are synchronistic with the time of your birth, when you took on separate existence, and they are synchronistic with your individuality in this life. They have much to say about you.

■ MYTH AND PSYCHOLOGY

The planets are named after the old gods and goddesses of Rome, which in turn link in with Greek and other pantheons. The planets represent 'life principles' – forces that drive the personality, and as such they can be termed 'archetypal'. This means that they are basic ideas, universal within human society and are also relevant in terms of the forces that, in some inexplicable way, inhabit the corners of the universe and inform the Earth and all human institutions. Thus the assertive energy that is represented by Mars means energetic action of all sorts – explosions and fires, wars, fierce debates and personal anger. Put briefly, here are the meanings of the planets:

- Mercury – intellect and communication
- Venus – love, unifying, relating
- Mars – assertion, energy, fighting spirit
- Jupiter – expansion, confidence, optimism
- Saturn – limitation, discipline
- Uranus – rebellion, independence
- Neptune – power to seek the ideal, sense the unseen
- Pluto – power to transform and evolve

These principles are modified according to the astrological sign they inhabit; thus Venus in Pisces may be gently loving, dreamy and self-sacrificing, while Venus in Aries will be demanding and adventurous in relationships. Thus the planets in signs form a complex psychological framework – and that is only part of the story of chart interpretation!

In the old mythologies these 'energies' or 'archetypes' or 'gods' were involved in classical dramas. An example is the story of Saturn and Uranus. Uranus is the rejecting father of Saturn, who later castrates and murders his father – thus innovative people reject reactionaries, who then murder them, so the revolutionary part of the personality is continually 'killed off' by the restrictive part. The exact positions and angles between the planets will indicate how this and other myths may come to life. In addition, the mere placement of planets by sign – and, of course, especially the Sun sign, call forth various myths as illustrations. The ancient myths are good yarns, but they are also inspired and vivid dramatisations of what may be going on repeatedly within your personality and that of your nearest and dearest. Myths are used by many modern psychologists and thera-pists in a tradition that has grown since Jung. We shall be using mythic themes to illustrate internal dynamics in this book.

SIGN	QUALITY	ELEMENT
Aries	Cardinal	Fire
Taurus	Fixed	Earth
Gemini	Mutable	Air
Cancer	Cardinal	Water
Leo	Fixed	Fire
Virgo	Mutable	Earth
Libra	Cardinal	Air
Scorpio	Fixed	Water
Sagittarius	Mutable	Fire
Capricorn	Cardinal	Earth
Aquarius	Fixed	Air
Pisces	Mutable	Water

■ THE SIGNS OF THE ZODIAC

There are twelve signs, and each of these belongs to an Element – Earth, Fire, Air or Water, and a Quality – Cardinal, Fixed or Mutable. The Cardinal signs are more geared to action, the Fixed tend to remain stable and rooted, whereas the Mutable signs are adaptable, changeable.

Jung defined four functions of consciousness – four different ways of perceiving the world – 'thinking', 'feeling', 'sensation' and 'intuition'. Thinking is the logical, evaluative approach that works in terms of the mind. Feeling is also evaluative, but this time in relation to culture and family needs. This is not the same as emotion, although 'feeling' people often process emotions more smoothly than other types. Jung saw 'feeling' as rational, too. 'Sensation' refers to the 'here and now', the five physical senses, while 'intuition' relates to the possible, to visions and hunches. Jung taught that we tend to have one function uppermost in consciousness, another one or maybe two secondary and another repressed or 'inferior', although we all possess each of these functions to some degree.

Jungian ideas are being refined and expanded, and they are incorporated into modern methods of personality testing, as in the Myers-Briggs test. If a prospective employer has recently given you such a test, it was to establish your talents and potential for the job. However, the basic four-fold division is still extremely useful, and I find that it is often of great help in assisting clients to understand themselves, and their partners, in greater depth – for we are all apt to assume that everyone processes information and applies it in the same way as we do. But they don't! It is worthy of mention that the important categories of 'introverted' and 'extraverted' were also identified by Jung. In astrology, Fire and Air signs seems to be extraverted, generally speaking, and Earth and Water introverted – and this has been borne out by the statistical research of the astrologer, Jeff Mayo. However, this doesn't mean that all feeling and sensation people are introverted and all intuitive and thinkers extraverted – this is definitely not the case, and calls for more detailed examination of the chart (e.g. lots of Fire and Water may mean an extravert feeling type).

Very broadly speaking we may link the Fire signs to intuition, Water to feeling, Earth to sensation and Air to thinking. Often thinking and feeling are drawn together and sensation and intuition are attracted, because they are opposites. This probably happens because we all seek to become more whole, but in the process can be painful. The notion of the four functions, when understood, does help to throw light on some of the stumbling blocks we often encounter in relationships. However, some people just do not seem to fit. Also Fire doesn't always correspond to intuition, Water to feeling, etc. – it seems this is usually the case, but not all astrologers agree. Some link Fire with feeling, Water with intuition, and most agree that other chart factors are also important. As with all theories, this can be used to help, expand and clarify, not as a rigid system to impose definitions. We shall be learning more about these matters in relation to the Sun sign in the following pages.

■ THE PRECESSION OF THE EQUINOXES

One criticism often levelled at astrology is that 'the stars have moved' and so the old signs are invalid. There is some truth in this, and it is due to a phenomenon called 'The Precession of the Equinoxes'. The beginning of the sign Aries occurs when the Sun is overhead at the equator, moving northwards. This is called the Spring Equinox, for now day and night are equal all over the globe, and the first point of Aries is called the 'equinoctial point'. Because the Earth not only turns on its axis but 'rocks' on it (imagine a giant knitting needle driven through the poles – the Earth spins on this, but the head of the needle also slowly describes a circle in space) the 'equinoctial point' has moved against the background of stars. Thus, when the Sun is overhead at the equator, entering Aries, it is no longer at the start of the constellation of Aries, where it occurred when the signs were named, but is now in the constellation of Pisces. The 'equinoctial point' is moving backwards into Aquarius, hence the idea of the dawning 'Aquarian age'.

So where does that leave astrology? Exactly in the same place, in actuality. For it all depends on how you think the constellations came to be named in the first place. Did our ancestors simply look up and see the shape of a Ram in the sky? Or did they – being much more intuitive and in tune with their surroundings that we are – feeling sharply aware of the quality, the energies around at a certain time of the year, and *then* look skywards, translating what they sensed into a suitable starry symbol? This seems much more likely – and you have only to look at the star groups to see that it takes a fair bit of imagination to equate most of them with the figures they represent! The Precession of the Equinoxes does not affect astrological interpretation, for it is based upon observation and intuition, rather than 'animals in the sky'.

■ USING THIS BOOK

Reach Your Potential – Libra explores your Sun sign and what this means in terms of your personality; the emphasis is on self-exploration. All the way through, hints are given to help you to begin to understand yourself better, ask questions about yourself and use what you have to maximum effect. This book will show you how to use positive Libran traits to your best advantage, and how to neutralise negative Libran traits. Don't forget that by reading it you are consenting, however obliquely, to the notion that you are connected in strange and mysterious ways to the web of the cosmos. What happens within you is part of a meaningful pattern that you can explore and become conscious of, thereby acquiring greater influence on the course of your life. Let this encourage you to ask further questions.

Some famous Librans

Julie Andrews, Brigitte Bardot, Sarah Bernhardt, Charles Boyer, T. S. Eliot, Mahatma Gandhi, George Gershwin, Graham Greene, Rita Hayworth, Charlton Heston, Deborah Kerr, John Lennon, Franz Liszt, Nietsche, Eleanor Roosevelt, Oscar Wilde, Bruce Springsteen, Bob Geldof, Sarah Ferguson (Duchess of York), Christopher Reeve, Katherine Mansfield, Chuck Berry, Cliff Richard, Bryan Ferry, Marc Bolan.

Bland, Balanced, or Beautiful – what sort of Libra are you?

Here is a quiz to give an idea of how you are operating at the moment. Its tone is light-hearted, but the intent is serious and you may find out something about yourself. Don't think too hard about the answers; just pick the one that appeals to you most.

1. **You enter a room and find that two of your good friends are arguing heatedly. What do you do?**

   a) ☐ Go out again, and make sure that you don't come back until they have finished.

   b) ☐ Go in and make determined conversation about the beauty of the view from the window so that they have to stop arguing and talk pleasantries.

   c) ☑ Take the trouble to enter the argument, displaying the merits of the points of view of each.

2. **Two separate groups of friends have organised an outing on the same day and you have been included in both. You find both of the plans equally appealing. How do you decide?**

   a) ☐ It really is appalling to have to face the physical limitation of only being in one place at one time. You tell both that you are going and end up present at the outing organised by your pushiest friend/the outing where you were offered a lift/the outing that started latest.

   b) ☐ You can't decide, so you get your best friend to decide for you. (The only trouble here is that you can't decide who is your *very* best friend . . .)

   c) ☑ You think about the pros and cons and weigh everything up. It is a nuisance, but you do come to a decision and inform people in good time. After all, it's only fair.

3. **You are asked your opinion on something that is important to the questioner. So you:**

   a) ☐ Change the subject. You aren't sure what the questioner thinks and you don't want to cause offence. For your part, you aren't sure. You can see merits in several viewpoints.

   b) ☐ You give an extended reply, punctuated by 'howevers' and 'on the other hands' so obscuring the original question.

   c) ☐ You ask the *questioner's* opinion.

4. **It is your mother-in-law's birthday party and she has cooked a special meal. To your horror you find that there is liver on your plate – and it's the one thing you abhor, but you hate the thought of being rude. What is to be done?**

   a) ☐ You swallow huge pieces without chewing or tasting, and chatter brightly to cover the greenness of your complexion. Then you wash down the disgusting mess with an extra glass or two of the excellent claret.

   b) ☐ You contemplate slipping the meat to the dog, but realise that it would be just *dreadful* if you were spotted. So you force down half and leave the rest, explaining charmingly that your hostess has been too generous, such a lovely meal, and so much of it.

   c) ☐ You explain clearly and politely that liver and you don't get on. You praise the rest of the meal intelligently, noticing choice of herbs and wine to complement. No one is in the least offended and you can tuck into the zabaglione – and compliment that!

5. **For your anniversary your dear friend gives you the ugliest flower vase in the universe. She lives locally and pops round regularly – how can you avoid causing offence?**

   a) ☐ You thank her effusively, and when she has gone you stuff the thing behind the sofa. Every time the doorbell rings you run to get the vase out.

b) ☐ You tell her that sadly the cat broke the vase. Trouble is, *she buys you another!*

c) ▣ You explain you do not have the place to show it off downstairs. However, upstairs, in your private study, is the very spot . . .

6. **You suspect your lover is seeing someone else – it's those unexplained absences, new clothes chosen without you, and those little gestures of togetherness are drying up. How do you deal with it?**

a) ☐ You go all manic – parties, outings, laughing, flirting – anything to get some attention and to take your mind off it.

b) ▣ You quietly continue as if nothing has happened 'Least said, soonest mended' and whatever it is will soon blow over.

c) ☐ Nothing could be worse than this breakdown in communication. You plan a quiet time where you can talk and find out what is really happening.

7. **At work you opt to move to a new department that has been created, but instead of being more interesting the work is boring and repetitive and you hate the fact you have now been given an office to yourself. How do you cope?**

a) ☐ You spend most of your time chatting to colleagues, and as little as possible at your lonely desk. You would like to go back to your old department, but you're afraid to jeopardise your career.

b) ▣ You buy flowers for the office and do the job as best you can (and you take long coffee breaks). Maybe another move will come up soon.

c) ☐ You take your boss a cup of coffee and a biscuit and discuss how to extend the scope of your job.

8. On a crowded train you find yourself sitting opposite a misbehaving child whose mother keeps hitting him and using bad language. So you:

a) ☑ Move. You'd rather stand in a draughty corridor.

b) ☐ Resolutely bury yourself in the *Times* crossword or Jane Austen's *Emma*.

c) ☐ Talk to the child and try to calm him down.

9. The relationship is over and you are both facing the fact. Your lover is moving out. What happens now?

a) ☐ You let your old lover keep a key and leave some stuff at your place. Then you find your old lover has dropped in for a quick shower and used the last of your milk for a cup of coffee. It's awkward.

b) ☐ The most important thing is that you stay friends and you work hard at this.

c) ☑ It isn't fair to hang on, but you will do your best to finish amicably.

Now count up your score. What do you have most of – a's, b's or c's?

Mostly a's. At the moment you are rather the 'bland' sort of Libra. You will bend over backwards to maintain harmony, fit in, cause no offence. The trouble is that you are getting lost in all of it – in fact, you probably can't remember what you really think, let alone feel – or did you ever know anyway? Remind yourself that you have the right to your own opinions and preferences, and the world won't come to an end if someone is just a little put out once in a while.

Mostly b's. You are the 'balanced' type, and while that does sound very laudable it means sacrifices – of your individuality as much as anything. How often do you feel irritated at having put yourself in an uncomfortable position through prioritising the comfort of others? You know what you want and think and it may be worth scattering the pigeons sometimes for the sake of your inner balance – which may be lacking.

Mostly c's. You are the 'beautiful' type of Libra, and you have the gift of getting your own way and keeping everyone else happy also. You are using your native skills very well, but remember you can't please *all* of the people *all* of the time. Some won't trust you. That's their problem, so don't be drawn into further compromise.

If you found that in many cases none of the answers seemed anywhere near to fitting you, then it may be that you are an uncharacteristic Libra. This may be because there are factors in your astrological chart that frustrate the expression of your Sun sign, or it may be because there is a preponderance of other signs outweighing the Libra part. Whatever the case may be, your Sun-sign potential needs to be realised. Perhaps you will find something to help ring a few bells in the following pages.

1

The essential Libra

The good is the beautiful

Plato

*The mighty abstract idea I have of beauty in all things
stifles the more divided and minute domestic happiness*

Keats

■ FAIR AND CHARMING

Libras are well known as the Princes and Princesses Charming of the
zodiac. Popular Libra is grace, beauty, justice and good manners
through and through, the true darling of every dinner party and
diplomatic function, the most perfect of partners, the fairest of friends
– and good-looking, to boot. Clearly people either adore Libra or hate
them for their sheer perfection, and many people do both at once.
Not that you Libras would ever accept that – after all, it hardly makes
sense, and to this Air sign, things do have to be rational. However,
Libra could spend an entertaining half-hour discoursing on the pros
and cons of love and hate – but that is another story . . . .

Sceptics and students of human nature might wonder whether all this
sweetness and light is truly possible. Can anyone be so perfect? Well,
you Libras will certainly try. This, rather than Virgo the Pragmatist, is
the perfectionist of the zodiac. Realists may assert that perfection is
not possible, but Libra, despite being logical, is rarely a realist – you
are idealists, none more so. The trouble with attempting perfection is
that along the way you may become a little too detached, indecisive or
naive. The angelic first impression is tarnishing – perhaps Libras are
human after all!

■ LIBRA BODY LANGUAGE

Libra strong in the natal chart often does bestow grace, and where physical beauty is lacking Libras are often expert at compensating. This is, after all, the sign of the Balance. Where the nose is a little large, Libra will style the hair to compensate. Legs too short? This is easily remedied by the right shoes. Perhaps a little overweight? This is expertly dealt with by choice of clothes.

Libra knows how to slouch gracefully. Often you arrange yourselves in your seats with obvious, but unselfconscious care for appearance. You have poise. Usually Libras are attentive – you watch others, and listen while they speak, giving at least the appearance of interest (although you may argue later) and there will usually be a twinkle in the eye, or a dazzling smile, designed to charm others – for to most Libras charm is second nature. Your body language is usually open – feet a little apart, arms welcoming, fingers spread, although this will be greatly modified by other chart factors. Movements are characteristically flowing and even stylised, although there can be an awkwardness, or a stiffness about Libra, which comes from continually bruising idealistic elbows against rough realities.

■ MYTHS OF THE SCALES

Libra, the Scales, is the only inanimate object found in the zodiac. It may, at first, seem very strange that the sign of relationships and love should be a 'thing', when all the others are colourful animals or people; in fact, this has great significance for Libra, as we shall see later. Libras, even when disinterested in astrology, are often intensely proud of this symbol of justice and equity, and many are quite emphatic that the symbol of the Scales should be in balance, not tilting at a crazy angle, as sometimes portrayed.

Myths about scales do not extend to very ancient times, and the most appropriate story concerns the weighing of the dead against the feather of Maat, in Egyptian mythology. Maat was the goddess of truth and cosmic order, and she took the form of an ostrich feather, placed on one pan of the scales of Osiris, god of the Underworld. In the opposite pan was placed the heart – or some say the soul – of the deceased person, and if the heart was heavier than the feather, then the deceased was not free to roam where he or she wished among gods and humans, but must return to Earth, to successive incarnations, until he or she had acquired the lightness and the rightness that would enable the deceased to progress.

Maat is truly goddess of cosmic order, which is rather different from human order, having more the meaning of inescapable and inexorable natural law. However, Maat did not condemn – her assessment was gentle and her decree wise. This is deeply important to Libra, who must avoid seeking a rather artificial order of the conceptual, the manufactured or the idealistic – codified laws, instead of the instinctual and innate law of the cosmos. Libras seeking true wisdom need to go beyond the 'truth of the head' to the 'truth of the heart', for only in this way is the heart light enough for Maat. And so the goal of Libran logic is to realise that logic will only ever go so far, and to achieve the balance that comes from accepting this.

■ ELEMENT, QUALITY AND RULING PLANET

We have seen that each of the signs of the zodiac belongs to one of the elements, Earth, Fire, Air or Water, and one of the Qualities, Cardinal, Fixed or Mutable. Libra is Cardinal Air. This means that Libras are orientated towards action, because of the cardinality, which is interesting, because you are famed for your indecisiveness.

However, Libran indecision is based on the need for action, where as Piscean indecision, for instance, may be based on quite the opposite. Given time, Libra will indeed arrive at a logical decision and proceed on the basis of it – unless the far preferable opinion of getting someone else to decide is achieved!

The fact that Libra is one of the Air signs is also interesting, for Air, as we have seen, has some thing in common with what Jung called the 'thinking' function. Thinking, of course, is something we all do, but in those where the 'thinking function' is strongest, logic is generally employed to evaluate life and its processes. Thinking people tend to believe that everyone should say what they mean and mean what they say, which is fine as far as Libran attachment to truth and justice is concerned. However, 'thinking' types often mistrust emotion and dislike displays of feeling, dismissing them as irrational, and when it comes to relationships, this can put Libra on shaky ground indeed. The truth is that Libra, sign of love and relating, is far more interested in the idea of relationship, the courtly postures, the graceful pas-de-deux. When it comes to sweaty grappling and tears, you would far rather retreat, back to the ivory tower. Of all Libran dilemmas – and they number not a few – this is perhaps the greatest, and we shall be examining this in more detail later on.

Libra is the seventh sign of the zodiac, and the second of the Air trinity. Fiery Aries the Pioneer begins the cycle, followed by Earthy Taurus the Farmer and Settler. Next comes Airy Gemini, sign of the Thinker and Communicator, followed by Watery Cancer of the Tribe and Family, and Leo, sign of the Monarch, the second Fire sign. Virgo, the second Earth sign, comes next, bringing the process of Reaping and Sorting, and now we arrive with Libra, sign of Relationship and Balance.

In the zodiacal circle Libra is opposite to Aries, and where Aries has a 'me-first' attitude, Libra focusses on the desires and wishes of others, and so the round of experience takes shape.

In the Northern Hemisphere the start of Libra marks the Autumn Equinox, where day and night are equal all over the globe, but in the North, dark is gaining. Some say that this is the turning of an unseen tide, when the veil between this world and that of the spirits is thin. Truly the 'balance' of reality is delicate. Now we have the harvest time and the acceptance that from death comes life, and life turns to death, and in respect of 'cosmic order' these are Libran themes. However, for those of you who live in the Southern Hemisphere, this is the Spring Equinox, when sunshine grows, vegetation comes to life and thoughts turn to love and pair-bonding, and this can be seen as the lighter, most alluring side of Libra.

Each sign is said to have a 'Ruling Planet'. This means that there is a planet that has a special affinity with the sign, whose energies are most at home when expressed in terms of that sign. The Ruling Planet for Libra is Venus, planet and goddess of love. Venus also rules Taurus but here we find her in a very different style. Libran Venus is aesthetic rather than seductive, artistic rather than fertile. Of course, she is still concerned with the delights of relating, and it is the purpose of most Librans to find the beauty and poise of the goddess in some walk of life and to bring this into their relationships, thoughts and creations.

■ THE DOVE OF PEACE

The dove is one of the birds associated with Aphrodite – the Greek counterpart to Venus – and billing and cooing doves are synonymous with peace and love. Libra is certainly the peacemaker. As the sign of the Balance one of your missions in life is to restore harmony wherever you find discord and many Libras are talented diplomats and tacticians. You love to pour oil on troubled waters. 'The quiet answer turneth away wrath' – you will not often respond aggressively to an attack, for you prefer to use your mind and your smooth tongue. If a schism has occurred, you will be the first to offer the olive branch, and if two people are at odds you will adroitly show each they are valued and 'right' in some context, finding the middle ground where agreement can be established.

However, strange as it may sound, this is also the sign of war. Nothing could be further from peace than war, so how can this sign of Balance possibly have anything to do with vicious conflict? The key lies in the use of that very word 'balance'. Somewhere inside Libra recognises the need for the balance of opposing forces, and this may tempt you to take the role of Devil's advocate. Some Libras thrive on argument and can be quite bossy. It can be fascinating to watch cool Libra setting the cat amongst the pigeons, and even more fascinating when Libra, having blown up a storm, performs a neat volte-face to agree with the original point of view.

Air signs are sometimes good at taking the moral high ground and attributing their little excesses to the irrationality of partners, and while this may not sound very nice on the face of it, it does result from a true detestation of emotional upsets. However, running away from unpleasantness may mean finding a superficial rather than a natural harmony. A Libra who is able to acknowledge this side of human nature achieves a true and deep balance that is best portrayed by the Yin and Yang – symbol of cosmic totality.

■ THE IVORY TOWER

Libran idealism can strive very hard to create heaven on Earth. However, it can also result in you shutting yourself up in an ivory tower where you close behind you the doors of perception to preserve the dogmas you have embraced as being the divine formulae. Yes, I did say 'dogmas'. You are lovers of fairness, who listen always to every side of the story, but you may become deaf in one ear when it comes to your cherished paradigm. Take this slice of 'truth' off the scales and everything wobbles. To this sort of Libra balance isn't a question of delicate poise, but of rigidity and the ivory tower is a calcified structure rather more like a prison than anything celestial.

Fair and just Libras may need to remind yourselves that your ideals cannot be condensed or codified, because then you are simply no longer ideal, but real and imperfect. Graven images are solid, cold and often ugly. In the words of Kahlil Gibran in *The Prophet* '. . . he who defines his conduct by ethics imprisons his song-bird in a cage'. If you can remember that truth wears many faces and that perfection lies in the imperfect, then you are capable of creating a true beauty that is subtle and inward.

■ MIRROR, MIRROR . . .

Approval is deeply important to Libra. Your talent for compromise extends even to compromising yourself on occasion, saying 'yes' when 'no' far better suits your schedule or preference. Libras do hate to be alone. Those with a strong Libran content to the chart always prefer to act as part of a couple – it is almost as if they find their identity in the presence of another. Because of this, Libra has been accused of hypocrisy, insincerity and generally being a 'pleaser'. Your Libran head nods like a blossom on a stem, and as you pick out salient points from the arguments of others with which you can concur, they just know, deep down that you could equally well find something attractive in the opposite viewpoint, and indeed would, if it were put to you. If others want the passionate commitment of 'you and me against the world' Libran graciousness can leave them feeling strangely high and dry. However, it is unfair to call Libra two-faced – you genuinely can't help seeing something of merit in most viewpoints, and there is no harm in a bit of tact. You like to be liked, and surely that is better than causing strife.

As far as it goes, that has much to recommend it. However, there is a danger with some Libras that a charming need for approval can become a search for identity, where Libra feels real and good only when you can see your reflection in the adoring eyes of someone else. And one pair of eyes is not convincing enough. You may collect admirers like precious stones in which you can catch a glimpse of yourselves reflected rosily back, and for a priceless moment feel valued and adored. This can happen to many of us, but here it is perhaps more of a hazard, for no one is more a 'people person' than Libra.

Feeding the vanity of such a Libra can be a bit like being eaten alive, piecemeal. First of all others are trapped by your flattery, charm and seduction, fattened up by attention and compliments until they are bursting with conviction– so juicy to Libra – that this is the most attractive and charming person they have ever met, and they are almost ready to lay down at your feet. Then come the little mix-ups, the broken dates, the phone that stays silent when they pick it up, absences explained too smoothly. Where their hair, figure and clothes were once lyricised, now they are damned with faint praise. Then their best friend tells them that their special love has been seen out with someone else.

Will it end here? Not likely! Having mustered the strength to end it all, Libra disarms them with plausible explanations and seductive compliments, just like in the beginning, and it all starts again . . . and again . . . and again. It is entirely possible, even probable, that there are several more lovers strung through the Libran life like a necklace. Libra may do this with friends as well as lovers – it's called keeping people on a string. Children also can be used as a mirror for Libran ideals. Tender-hearted Libras may flatter rather than cause hurt, but the Libra we are considering here is concerned only with his or her own feelings, which are very sad and needy indeed. Others may not feel at all special knowing that they are one of a group, but believe me they are, in their way. Libra needs them, in order to feel worthwhile.

This sounds a real problem, and indeed it can feel that way. However, it is far worse for this sort of Libra who feels eternal yearning and dissatisfaction. After all, having seen the light others can walk away, mourn and seek something with more depth, but Libra is doomed to search forever for their own reflection, and like vampires of gothic myth, they have none. What is to be done?

If you recognise yourself even just a little bit in any of the above you need only to call on your sense of balance, truth and fairness to assure you that whatever friends and lovers can give you, it cannot be a sense of being truly worthwhile, deep inside, and that can come only from inner convictions. If you are one of those Libras who collects 'mirrors' to hang on your wall, you need to realise that you will never, ever see your true self reflected, and that can be glimpsed only by turning inwards, perhaps towards what feels like a void, and staunchly looking into it. Eventually, you will see something worth much more than admiration and approval, and you will approve of yourself. That is really valuable, and it is genuine and – balanced.

The 'mirror' does have positive aspects, too. The gift of seeing ourselves as others see us is to become impartial observers of our own failings and virtues, and this is a Libran talent. As long as the balancing factor extends also to the opinions of others, who may, after all, not be right, and as long as Libra does not find *rasion d'être* in these opinions, but seeks rather to weigh them against other impressions, this can lead only to greater wholeness.

■ WHEN THE SCALES TILT

Libra is a most cultured sign. One Libran lady, informing a friend that her daughter had just had her first baby, was met with the reply 'Oh, but you are much too refined to be a grandmother!' She took this as a great compliment. There can be just a trace of snobbery in Libra, and it is almost as if this sign originated in such rarefied realms that it is too much to be required to cope with the mundanities of everyday life. Our clue lies in the 'inanimate' nature of the Scales. There is much about the ordinary and the human – not to mention the animal – that Libra may find most offensive from greasy pans to bad grammar. Libra may stand for hours in a supermarket debating whether or not to buy a kumquat. It's not the decision that's so gruelling, although that's bad enough (maybe pears would be more economical, and then the children like bananas … but they are so ordinary …). It's the very banality of everyday quandaries that some Libras can find so boring that it is a struggle even engaging with them.

Every Libra needs style and glamour. You need the opportunity to place your creative hands on something that will satisfy your need for beauty. The aesthetic, the cultured and the peaceful must become part of Libra's life. Of course, not all Libras spend their lives at garden parties and art galleries – plenty are found on building sites, in kitchens and factories. Not all are noticeably 'refined' by any means. One Libran young man I know likes nothing better than to wrestle with his nephews. And he also consumes baked beans and beer in considerable quantity with predictable results! However, the point here is that, far from being repelled, everyone finds him pleasant and amusing, and they respond to his good humour and warmth. Coarse? Well, yes, sometimes. But offensive? Never!

Libra must have the opportunity to balance the banal with the transcendent, the workday with the relaxing, and there must be some corner in each day when you can 'leave it all behind'. For many

Libras philosophy or fine music give them their slice of heaven: for others it can be looking their best and behaving like a gracious aristocrat – a part which many Libras take to like a cat to cream. Still others find what they need is to be in the company of friends, with whom they are generally popular. Without something of the sublime to balance the ridiculous in the human condition, the Libran Scales start to tilt at a crazy angle. Forced up against the grubby and the prosaic, Libra may insist upon discussing the relative merits of the Impressionists versus the Expressionists with the plumber, or become unable to scramble an egg without recourse to French phrases. Nothing makes Libra cranky more quickly than a life of disillusionment. If you are a Libra, ensure that you lift your nose off the grindstone and into the gracious at regular intervals, and make the cultured, however you define it, part of your daily life, not something you have to beg, borrow or pretend at stolen intervals. If you care for a Libra, then give them their share of elegant living, even if you do not really understand why bangers and mash offend them so. Maybe the divine scent of hyacinths for the soul will waft your way, too.

Echo and Narcissus

Greek legend tells of the nymph Echo, who fell in love with a beautiful youth called Narcissus. Narcissus is very much a Libran figure, for he was extremely attractive and charming. Every girl who met him admired him, and many fell deeply in love with him. However, Narcissus could find no one who he could truly love.

Not only did mortal women love the beautiful youth: the nymphs of the trees and glades loved him also. The nymph Echo loved him especially and desperately. Her plight was saddest of all, for the goddess Hera had punished Echo for distracting her with her sweet voice while Hera's divine husband, Zeus, philandered. Hera had condemned Echo never to be able to speak, except for repeating the last words anybody addressed to her. Trying to tell Narcissus of her love, she only succeeded in irritating and puzzling him, and so she fled away into the forest in despair. At length she faded away until all that remained was her voice, that, to this day, still calls out to the traveller in lonely and rocky places.

Meanwhile Narcissus became more and more vain, and because of his self-absorption the love goddess, Aphrodite, decided to punish him. While out walking, Narcissus caught sight of himself in a still pool. He was transfixed! Never had he seen so beautiful a face. He knelt to touch its perfection, but his hand stirred the water so he lost sight of it. Motionless he knelt, bent over the pool, choking on tears of yearning that he knew would only fall into the water and disturb the vision. No one could persuade him to move, so caught was he by the curse of Aphrodite; so in love with his own image. Day was followed by night, and in turn by pale dawn. Narcissus did not move, he could not bear to. Night came again and the moonlight turned Narcissus to an alabaster statue. Then the Sun came up, but it did not warm him. At length the beautiful youth was no more, and in his place grew a flower – the narcissus, which ever since has adorned watersides.

Like most tales this has a lot of meanings. It tells of the dangers of excessive self-love that is not based on reality, for 'falling in love' with one's image is far from appreciating one's true potential. Echo's fate hints at the dangers of using the beautiful as a distraction, and the entire story speaks of loss of identity in pursuit of what is attractive, but empty. However, it also tells how the tragic and the meaningless can be turned into something exquisite, as Narcissus is turned into a lovely flower that blooms eternally. Libra may lose sight of deeper values in pursuit of the elegant and lovely, but no one has a greater talent for creating what is enduringly beautiful. 'A thing of beauty is a joy forever' as every Libra knows so well.

■ PRACTICE AND CHANGE ■

- You must have something lovely, stylish, cultured and glamourous as part of your daily diet. Introduce balance in this, as in all else. You are entitled to your hyacinths for the soul. Cultivate them along with carrots and potatoes, and have the courage of your convictions.

- Do not allow your idealism to ossify into a lifeless plaster-cast, even in the privacy of your soul. Always be open to new truths and new beauties – they amount to the same thing.

- Try always to be true to yourself and if you are not quite sure what that means for you, make it the business of your keen mind to find out. It is fine to compromise on a super-ficial level and probably you will always wish to be polite and conciliating. However, this should not extend to the point where you feel good or worthwhile only when you are pleasing somebody else. Please yourself.

- Make your charm work for you. You can use your 'charm' specifically, as a diplomat, peacemaker or tactician, in a way that will bring you fulfilment. You can use your sense of what pleases others to create an environment that is pleasurable for you, not one in which you have to have all the compromises.

- Some may call you indecisive, but that is because you see things from all angles, and that is a talent. Where you do not have to decide, be prepared to sit – elegantly – upon the fence. Where decisions do have to be made you may need to employ strategies to avoid wasting time and per-haps money. Make a list of the pros and cons and give yourself plenty of time to mull it over, while doing other things. Don't leave a decision until the last minute.

- In your pursuit of harmony, remember to leave space for some of the turbulent emotions that we all have to deal with.

2 ♎ Relationships

And when Love speaks, the voice of all the gods
Make heaven drowsy with the harmony

Shakespeare, *Love's Labour's Lost*

It is said that all the world loves a lover, and that may be one of the reasons why Libra is such a popular sign. Love is Libra's principal preoccupation, and you often consider yourself highly sexed and deeply romantic. Loneliness is something that those with a strong Libra content to the chart try to avoid at all costs, for you simply do not feel complete without a partner. How can all the peace and beauty that this world has to offer be appreciated to the full without another to share it with? Songs are not the same without the harmony, and the wonder of sunset, the magic of moonlight and the moods of the ocean lose their soul when observed through solitary eyes. Love not only makes the world go round, but it has the power to change it, and Libra senses this. This sign has the gift of seeing the beauty in another and reflecting it back.

Libras can be fervent and even poetical. Many of you certainly walk off with first prize for flirtatious remarks or sexy *double entendres* – all delivered with a slanting glance capable of weakening both the knees and the defences of the opposite sex. So this Venus-ruled sign must be the steamiest, most erotic and abandoned lover in the zodiac, right? Well, no, not really, because human nature is not that simple and Libra is far from being a simple sign in any respect, certainly not where the emotions are concerned. For this is an Air sign, and Air signs are concerned with concepts, ideas, ideals and principles. All of this sits uncomfortably with the savagery and messiness of encounters between even the most civilised of humans. After all, we are all animals in part. Libra, sign of the inanimate Balance, would like to believe that we are all celestial. Humanity is bad enough. As for the bestial – leave that back in the caves, please.

What really fascinates Libra, often occupying the greater part of your waking thoughts (and probably plenty of your dream-time, too) is the *idea* of love. A Libra I know well often asks 'What is love?' and between us we come up with a different answer every time. Libra will debate and ponder the essence of love and the ethics and practices surrounding it until the cows come home and mate in the meadow – but that certainly won't supply any answers! However, it isn't merely the principles involved that occupy Libra – this sign gets off on the romantic ideal, the sublimity, the blissful perfection of it all. It doesn't take much thought to realise that this is asking for trouble, and, human beings being what they are, trouble is what poor Libra all too often finds.

That Libra refinement comes into play in the arena of love. One couple, both Libras, only 'talk dirty' in French, presumably because it isn't quite *so* dirty that way. Ritual is extremely important to these people and, despite their vivid fantasies and preoccupation with erotic imagery, sexually Libra can be about as hard to start as an old car on a frosty morning. However, in the case of Libra, it's definitely a plush Rolls Royce with velvet seats and an engine that purrs like a sunbathing tiger once it gets going. Libras aren't built for slumming it, and while there are plenty of 'basic' Libras, they have the edge on the culture of their peers and there is something a touch rarefied about even the most rough and ready. A hint of old-fashioned courtesy, a love of music, an attention to comfort – it is all part of the Libran charm.

Two main stumbling blocks stub the graceful Libran toe, time and time again when they enter a relationship. One is the sad but simple fact that we are not celestial creatures. We do not alight in pristine splendour, straight from the nearest rosy cloud, and we do have BO, runny noses, spots, dandruff and dirty underwear. We do also have mundane concerns like shopping and tax returns that take our attention away from Mozart and Grand Marnier. A Libra once said 'I do wish the good lord had seen fit to place our genitals further away from our excretory organs', and so uttered a prayer for all of the sign.

The second and more tricky stumbling block is emotions. Feelings are lovely when they are about love, esteem, honour, admiration and desire for union with the beloved. Even lust can be poetical. Not so jealousy, envy, anger and hatred. Aware Libras lament that these exist and try to expunge them as far as possible from their lives. For the less aware or realistic they can mean tragedy. One Libran man, deeply in love with a woman other than his wife found his infidelity hard to cope with, but he managed to rationalise it. 'What she doesn't know won't hurt her. She's really left me no choice, the way she's been all these years', etc. – Libras are good at arguments such as these. What was too much for him, however, were the feelings of jealousy that he experienced about his lover's working companions and all of the life she had that he could not share. Unable to say 'I'm jealous and I can't bear it. What am I to do?' he invented complex arguments to 'prove' she was not faithful to him. 'I just know you have been seeing Steven, and nothing you say will convince me to the contrary,' he intoned, sternly. After this, to punish her (Libran love of balance extends almost to biblical retribution on occasion) he refused there-after ever to tell her he loved her. Sadly, their passionate love withered and died, although I don't believe either of them has ever quite recovered. Needless to say, his lover had never been unfaithful to him, by anyone's definition!

The dilemma of imperfect emotions is one that Libras have to resolve in some way if relationships are to work for them, and this is something that you do need to ponder. The thing is, there is no way of having a meaningful relationship without emotions and many Librans grow wise, if a little frayed at the edges grappling with this. You are generally honorable people who love to pay a compliment and hate to hurt feelings so much that you usually stay friends with old lovers – goodbye forever is almost an obscenity to you. This world is a little too crude, banal and squalid for you, but you give others a glimpse of how things can look from a dove's eye view, up in the blue.

■ LIBRAN SEXUALITY

Libras thinks a lot about sex, they read about it, analyse it and imagine it. To many Libras there is nothing more wonderful than love between a man and a woman. However, when it comes to the point, the erotic scenarios that may have been constructed so exquisitely, can come between you and your responses. The lighting may be too harsh, everything may be happening too quickly or your lover may say something that doesn't have quite the romantic ring. Any lack of good taste or the smallest hint, even mistakenly, that you are not the epitome of glamorous desirability can turn you off before the 'on' switch has even been located.

Libra needs ritual in sex. The trouble with the word 'ritual' is that it can evoke the repetitious, automatic and mindless to modern ears, but that isn't at all the type of ritual that arouses Libra. The true sense of ritual is that it forms an outward sign of inner change and that it alters the state of mind so that true magic can take place. It takes more to evoke the transcendent than a few physical jerks, as you know only too well, and the real wonder of sex rests in the union of mind, spirit, body and soul that is brought about. This doesn't happen accidentally – things have got to be right. So you may go in for quite complex choreography, and indeed this can be self-defeating if spontaneity is lost. However, a little jasmine, a pale silk sheet, a shaft of moonlight and a compliment delivered with passionate sincerity can go a long way. Even further goes an attention to timing and a fine sense of the needs and responses of your partner. Libras are nothing if not considerate in bed, and you are usually very skilful. Yes, you will have thought a lot about the process, but you are far too graceful to move to a formula.

Because you set such a store by quality, it might be assumed that Libras never have quantity, but that isn't always the case. You do not like to say 'no' and can be a pushover for flattery. However, no one regrets the sordid more quickly than Libra, and the whole encounter may seem pretty empty if there is no chance for relationship. This doesn't mean that typical Libras make love only when they are *in* love – you are as capable of casual lust as the next person. However, it is usually important to 'stay friends'. To a partner deeply in love this dispassionate companionship may be much more cruel than total rejection, but kindness is the intention. You like to maintain a connection and a dialogue, and sometimes this can seem more important than physical satisfaction.

Libran ladies do need to be seen to be seductive in order to function at their best in bed. Ms Libra may remember to arrange her limbs to best advantage, or present her 'good' side when in the steamiest of situations. It's not that she's cool. Simply, to be aware of appearances is second nature to her, and she will make like Botticelli's Venus so you'd never notice the difference, when the Moon shines. Her responses are certainly thoughtful, and she can be surprisingly assertive between the sheets. She thinks about what will please and delivers it, like a true courtesan, to the man of her choice. One Libran lady I know described how she would simply adore a certain portion of her man's anatomy, verbally and by admiring gaze, because this is what turned him on. You might think that in the context of all that romantic idealism such might seem dry and tedious, but not so. Libra in love has the gift of taking delight in another's pleasure.

Mr Libra is often extolled as being the most adroit of lovers. Being a good lover turns him on and he watches the responses of his partners, matching himself to her and moving with her. Even when his heart is not engaged he is still aware of the 'partnership' element, and this, along with his talent for saying the right thing in *just* the right husky tone can make him a real heartbreaker. However, his sexuality is not as reliable as he might like it to be. Because Libra is an Air sign, the physical wheels roll only when the mind is in gear. Mr Libra can be one of the first to say that the human body, however lovely, is more beautiful clothed. An atmosphere, a suggestion, black lace and black leather may do far more than acres of bare flesh.

Libras of both sexes have the gift of both subtlety and passion – it's just a question of getting the balance right!

White Buffalo Woman

Ages ago, a supernatural woman brought a gift to the Oglala tribe, of the American Midwest. She first appeared to two young men, clad in white. One of them rushed to embrace her, overcome with lust for her beauty. She smiled and a soft white mist descended to cover their embraces. The other, realising that here was a goddess, held back in wonderment. When the mist withdrew all that remained of his companion was a skeleton. The goddess explained that this man had obtained what he sought.

Then she went with the second man to his village where she instructed the elders in the making of the pipe of peace. This pipe represents the union of the feminine, as represented by the bowl, with the masculine, as portrayed by the stem. The smoke that travelled through them both was the infusion of Spirit. Urging the Oglala always to honour their mother, the Earth, the woman disappeared in the guise of a white buffalo.

Here we have a story that has meaning for Libra. Harmony and unity between male and female are accomplished in the pipe, which then becomes a vehicle for the transcendent. Those who appreciate this are blessed. For others who are too hasty or too superficial, the streak of ruthless justice that appears from time to time in Libra awards them with 'death' – not literal death, of course, but a death of the spirit. The gross and the earthbound are repellent to Libra. Finally the buffalo is a symbol of bounty, for this animal provided the native Americans with all they needed – flesh to eat, bones to make weapons and hide to make tents, shoes and clothes. To honour mother Earth and the life-giving buffalo shows a profound balance indeed. As with all tales of the native Americans this has many meanings. Here we have extracted some that are pertinent to Libra.

■ LIBRA WOMAN IN LOVE

Here we have a woman who can look as feminine as a pink bunny, giggling, flirting and preening, but make no mistake, underneath the soft and shining hair there is a mind like a Venus Flytrap missing nothing. Like all Air-sign women this lady thinks, and her thoughts are logical and thoroughly reasoned. She may not always be scientific or practical, but concepts are her field all the same. She is not easily impressed by a square jaw, and her heart is more readily melted by a broad mind than a pair of broad shoulders. If she is in love, or deeply attracted to a man, she will certainly acquiesce and adapt, but if time shows her that her admiration was unfounded, she can turn into a scathing critic. She likes skilful conversation, style, poetry and romance à la Barbara Cartland. Underneath her frills and lipstick she is often deeply feminist. Remember, this is the sign of equality, and Ms Libra is anybody's equal. However much she may be in love, she will give no man her respect who doesn't respect her.

Occasionally, Libran women do go for the crisply tailored approach or tramp around in patched dungarees, and this may be in the interest of redressing the balance between masculine and feminine. More likely, however, this lady makes like the epitome of the romantic heroine. She can be quite irresistible. Gentle, with a piquant charm and a bubbling wit, she is 'all woman' but when the chips are down she can turn her hand and mind to whatever is most useful. As a committed partner she is a huge asset, for she knows how to act the temptress. Besides, her catering is often faultless, her accounting a work of art and her talent for charming everyone from the bus driver to the boss-man worth more than a princess's dowry. Ms Libra is often the most sought-after in the zodiac.

However, princesses don't usually come without a price and it takes some hefty heroics to win them. Ms Libra will not expect her lover to make like the man in the Milk Tray advertisement, but in time it will become obvious that she does expect more than a cuddle and a pat on the rump. She does not like to be patronised. She needs buckets full of love, attention and compliments, and she must always be treated like the lady that she is. But she is, first and foremost, a human being with a brain, and anyone who forgets that is liable to get the sharp edge of her tongue. She needs to be spoken to – not just words of love. She's interested in news items, philosophy and what her lover's colleagues said. No modern woman will ever play second fiddle, but while some may smile indulgently at a little of the macho stuff, Ms Libra's seamless tact will rip ragged if there is a hint he does not regard her as truly equal. After a few of her well-turned phrases he may be the one to end up feeling inferior!

This lady, who can look as delicate as a rosebud, is quite capable of rolling up her organdie sleeves and getting down to some graft if the occasion calls for it. She can work out budgets to precision and still have some left over to buy fresh flowers – yes, she is capable and hard working. When making love she will be soft, responsive, inventive and initiatory, but always, always, womanly. She knows how to look delicious and cook even more deliciously. Deeply in love though she may be, there is always a part of her that is afraid to let go in case something ugly or uncontrollable – or just plain old human slips out. Faithful though she can certainly be, the attentions of just one man may never be quite enough, and while her love is given to one, her attention may extend to several as she collects admirers to convince herself she is desirable. Her lover should not take this too seriously or regard it as a threat, because it has nothing to do with her feelings for him. Finally, Ms Libra knows the real meaning of being a partner and will put everything into the role. However, she will never offer mindless adoration, and while she is loving her lover passionately she is also assessing him, rationally. If he can't cope with that, he'd better find a real fluffy bunny to cuddle – if he can face the boredom!

◼ LIBRA MAN IN LOVE

Women whose taste is for the Neanderthal are about thirty centuries too early for this man. The last thing Mr Libra wants to do is bop the opposition over the head with a club and drag his woman off by the hair. Of course, he can 'play rough' if he knows that's what turns her on, but his true style is one of gentleness and subtlety and he will woo her as much by fair words as deeds. It is often said that it is the tiny ingredient of the opposite sex, the tender touch coupled with the baritone, the hairy masculine arm cradling the baby, that is the most deeply and subtly arousing, and Mr Libra often embodies this naturally.

When this man is really in love, then his native idealism reaches the stratosphere. He will try to be rational, and sometimes he will burst the bubble of his lover's own dreams so that she is sure she's got hold of a stony pragmatist, but this isn't the case. Inside he is building castles in the air and a whole array of theories and plans that extend from the belief that this is the Love To End All Loves, and he has found the quintessence of partnership. Yes, there *is* something just a little impersonal about this, and it may seem sometimes as if he is more in love with the relationship and the idea of being together than he is with her, but it has enchantment, nonetheless.

A quick roll in the hay or romp on the sofa while babysitting are not really his style, although as he is as highly sexed as the next man he will often settle for this. However, he would far rather spend a leisurely evening over a lingering dinner and make love, equally leisurely, between scented sheets. Usually Mr Libra is a great respecter of women. As Ms Libra has affinity for the masculine role, in certain respects, Mr Libra often finds he can put himself in a woman's place and understand what she is feeling. Rarely does this render him effeminate – more usually he is a gentle and very sincere lover of the fair sex. No one takes to the role of 'toyboy' better than some Libras. Mr Libra is quite genuinely capable of appreciating the Feminine with real affection, at whatever age.

Libra can philander with the best, but he does not need to prove his masculinity by collecting notches on the bedpost. He is more concerned with building a relationship, talking about it, practising it and talking some more. No one puts more into love than Libra, and he tries his hardest to be fair and reasonable.

If his lover is unfaithful, Libra may surprise her by a violent reaction or a cold ruthlessness. This is not the jealousy of Scorpio, although Libra can, of course, be jealous and will hate himself for it. To Libra it isn't just him she has betrayed, it is his ideas. Somehow that hurts his emotions more, in an odd way. He may find it very hard to reinstate his image of the partnership if she has ruptured it, and he will find his self-esteem is fractured if he loses his cool, yells, shouts and rips clothing. If she wants to stay close to this man, she must love his standards as much as she loves him and she will be rewarded by the warmth and companionship of a mate who knows the true meaning of relating, on all levels. She will also have a man who will treat her as an equal, really talk to her and yet make love to her in such a way she will know who is Tarzan and who is Jane, even though the jungle is a thousand miles away.

■ GAY LIBRA

Libras often have a special sympathy for gays, and perhaps a little admiration, too. Gay men often exhibit a subtlety and culture that Libra values, and the entire concept of homosexuality may strike Libra as representing inner balance. The blind prophet of Greek myth, Tiresias, spent some time both as a man and a woman, thus gaining exceptional wisdom, and he has been linked to Libra. Libran women may be feminist, and while the more usual image is of soft femininity, this may be the 'iron hand in the velvet glove' – Margaret Thatcher, the 'Iron Lady' is a Libra. Alternatively, some Libran ladies can be decidedly 'butch' combining certain masculine characteristics and expressing vehemence about equality. Occasionally, Libran men can be effeminate. Thus, of all the signs, Libra, the 'love-sign' may have more cross-gender elements than most.

Of course, this does not mean that a greater proportion of Librans are homosexual than any other sign. What it may confer is self-acceptance in Libras who are gay. Concepts are important to Libra, and they will rarely find anything to offend their ideals in being gay. This sign, although not specifically rebellious, is not welded to the cultural norm. Libras usually have sufficient faith in their ability to charm themselves into the good books and drawing rooms of most people, regardless of sexual preference. Their fairness and open-mindedness stand them in good stead, whatever their sexual preference, or those of their companions.

■ LIBRA LOVE TRAPS

Sucker for flattery

The Air signs often take a while to discover how they really feel. They will go off and think about how they feel, how they ought to feel and how their partner feels, but when it comes to simply *feeling* they tend to get – well – confused. While Libra is rather better than Aquarius and Gemini when it comes to emotions, your ego is your Achilles' heel. You so badly need approval and admiration that being told you are lovely, as long as it is done moderately, convincingly and with judicious repetition, can short-circuit genuine feeling (or lack of it) and convince you that you are really in love. What you are really in love with is yourself, but even that is not genuine. Self-image at this point gets a little vague, mixed up with how your lover sees you, and all your lover actually gets is cupboard love. In truth a Libra who is manipulated this way is somewhat low on true self-esteem. Flattery like this can keep Libra on a string for years, and you may put up with behaviour that is otherwise quite abusive as long as things are levelled up by the right compliment, just in time. The longer this goes on, the deeper true self-esteem plummets. If you recognise yourself in this, it is time to cut the ties.

This can be deeply painful, for you are cutting yourself off from what feels like life support, but it isn't. This is destructive to you, and not about loving or relating, but rather about control – and that isn't fair. Set yourself free to find a real love, that warms your heart *and* flatters your vanity, in due measure.

Familiarity breeds contempt

If your eyes are permanently raised towards the divine image, it can be quite hard to look down and find that you are stuck up to the ankles in the mud of vulgarity. However, how can you have anything like an intimate relationship without finding hairs in the drain on occasion? Of course, most Libras have the common sense to cope with such things, and experience no problem. For some, however, the banal really is excruciating. They want the refinement, the flattery, the courtship and the starry eyes without having to face the fact that such things disappear like Cinderella's coach with the crude light and burnt toast of the following morning. Real relationships and true intimacy are based on encounter and partnership in every part of life, and the trick is to keep romance alive – something most Libras are very good at. Some struggle with this, however, and unless they can live in a mansion, with separate bedrooms and bathrooms meeting by appointment only when fully groomed – rather like the royalty of yore – then they just can't cope. Romances may start and founder, because illusions evaporate. This may leave Libra in the worst possible situation for this sign – lonely.

How can this be improved? Unless a partner with the same characteristics can be found, love at the end of a bargepole is unlikely to work. Perhaps some searching questions need to be asked. What is it that is so unacceptable about being ordinary and human? And what is so fearful about true intimacy? This isn't a matter of taste and refinement, it is a matter of avoiding something that needs to be faced. It may be worth making some sacrifices to find some answers, for the reward can be every Libra's dream – a relationship that really enhances life.

■ LIBRA AND MARRIAGE

Libras are the marrying kind and many do it several times – not intentionally, of course. Each time it's a 'forever kind of love' except that forever lasts only a few years when idealistic youth (and some Libras marry very young) turns into a rather more jaded, but still hopeful maturity. Of course, you may have to kiss a lot of frogs before you find a prince, but you aren't dabbling. Each time a serious effort is made, and when it fails you are shattered by your own fallibility. Many Libras are endlessly fascinated by the magic of man/woman relationship – one Libran singer calls marriage a 'mystery ride' and it's one for which Libras queue in excited anticipation. You may go in for 'serial monogamy' and, indestructible idealists that you are, you always believe that this time will be the last. Well, maybe it will. In the end, life deflates the castles in the air and then there is a chance of some solid foundations. You will certainly work at it.

We have said repeatedly that this is the sign of partnership and Libras do their best to be good partners, weighing all factors and trying to be fair, impartial and loving. You will usually take half the blame in a quarrel, as long as your partner shoulders the other half. Heap it all on your shoulders and you turn unco-operative and self-righteous, protesting your spotless innocence. What you do need to remember when making a serious contract is, first, to try to be realistic. Do you really love and honour this person or are you projecting on to them an image of how love should and could be? Well, it *could* be like that, but not with this person if he or she is grossly incompatible in most ways. Relationship is made up of two separate people, it isn't a perfect entity that descends upon a couple and makes them one.

Second, as a Libra, intellectual compatibility and harmony in tastes is more vital than sexual attraction or any other ingredient. As a Libra your mind is your most erogenous zone, and it is also the make-or-break site for the building of relationships. Take your time, weigh and balance to your heart's content, for this is one area where a little hesitation goes a long way. The old saying 'Marry in haste, repent at leisure' niggles at too many disaffected Libras. Never fear that you will be left on the shelf, for there is a scant chance of that. However, the shelf is a good temporary vantage point for seeing all sides.

■ WHEN LOVE WALKS OUT – HOW LIBRA COPES

Betrayal rips out the heart of Libras, for although you are not above flirting yourself, you are quite capable of separating this from your emotional life. Living amid the rubble of shattered dreams is a continual reminder of just how cruel and imperfect this world is, just when you thought you had found the magic formula for everlasting bliss. If your partner then refuses to see you, to discuss, communicate and at least maintain a friendship, this makes matters worse. Many people feel that a 'clean break' is best, but to most Libras it is not, and they are far better able to adjust if a platonic relationship – which is, after all, still a relationship – can survive. Bereft Libras do sometimes wallow in romantic yearning, idealising the lost love out of all proportion to their true merit. You cope best at this stage if friends rally round and introduce a little realism, where possible, without trampling too heavy on all the illusions. It is also far better for Libran self-respect if you have not lost your temper or your dignity. Sneakily, it may also help if you have got your own back or lev-elled the score in some way, and a past infidelity that caused you guilt may be a great consolation at this time, rather than a source of remorse. However, unless there are other chart factors that suggest morosity, you will not wallow forever. Mostly you are too popular, sought-after and amiable. Your ruler, the love-goddess shows you that life is a beautiful thing and you are, after all, 'beautiful people'.

Starting afresh

Libras not infrequently hurl themselves into a new relationship with a haste that would be indecent, were you not so plausible and gra-cious about it. The phrase 'on the rebound' springs to mind, but in a sense you are generally on the rebound from the dislike of being alone. Grande passion or convenient companionship, whatever your previous relationship you will need to replace it as soon as pos-sible, at least in youth. More mature Libras have more cultivated ideas about what they seek, and will be much more judicious.

It is of very little use to advise Libras to take some time alone, for only in rare cases are you able to enjoy this or make the best use of it. Yes, it can be lovely to be able to enjoy Schubert and smoked salmon if your philistine of an ex insisted on the Spice Girls and cod and chips, and more reserved Libras will certainly appreciate this. However, like most people, but even more than most, you need your friends now. You need to be talked sense to, gently. You need to be made to laugh – and cry, too, for many Libras, while expressing their loneliness, will still hold back the tears, and you need a mate to accompany you to your favourite places. A little matchmaking won't come amiss – you would certainly do this for your friends, given half a chance. If you are given the chance you are sure to live, to love again.

■ PRACTICE AND CHANGE ■

- You can't have a relationship without human beings, and human beings are by definition flawed when compared with fairytale. Do not let what is ugly or banal destroy your faith. Look beyond, not with blinkered eyes, but with eyes that see the whole picture, and try to love the imperfections, not in spite of them.

- Extending from the above, it is inevitable that unruly passions will find their way into any relationship that is of any moment. Try not to rationalise, patronise or deny – it's part of something meaningful and designed to help you learn more about yourself.

- Enjoy flattery if it comes your way, but never allow it to sway you into behaving in ways that you will later regret.

- You probably enjoy sexual experience that is somewhat stylised, and you may have a taste for erotica, from the elegant to the kinky. Don't be sidetracked by this into forgetting that the real point is relationship. It's not how you do it, it's who you do it with that counts.

- Be careful that you do not over-romanticise partners, especially when the relationship is over. If you thought they were *that* good, then you did not see them, you saw the reflection of your own fantasies.

- It may be hard for you really to 'let go' even when you are deeply in love. Remind yourself that the greatest gift you can give a partner is that of trust. Such is not just about sharing confidences, it is about showing the raw bits of your soul.

- Practise keeping romance alive actively, rather than dreaming about it and then being shocked by reality. Love is a creative act.

3 ♎ All in the family

I was brought up to be the person others wanted me to be, so that they would like me and not be bothered by my presence. When I began to be me, I felt that I had more to give

Liv Ullman

A Libran influence in the family is to be valued, for Libras have a strong sense of family as community. Your peacemaking talents come to the fore if there is discord, and you have the gift of bringing out the best in everybody. However, the view that Libra is always accommodating is not quite accurate, and those who know Libra intimately, within four walls, are aware that you can have your scratchy side, too.

■ LIBRA MOTHER

Libra mum rarely relishes the dirty nappy and runny-nose stage of childhood. She is only too happy when her children have reached the age where they can be reasoned with and when they are trained to be at least partly civilised. If possible, Libra mum will pass the bulk of the childcare to someone else, while she goes out to work or pursues some other more cultured pastime. Most Libran ladies like to have a career, and many are very successful. Libra mother is at her best in the studio or office – or indeed anywhere where there is adult interaction. Nothing will drive her crazy quicker than being stuck at home with the washing and baby talk. However, she always makes space later in the day to spend quality time with her children, helping them with homework, talking to them about their experiences and reading stories.

Libra mother is unlikely to choose to have a large family, unless she can afford full-time help. She can be quite stern with her children over behaviour she regards as unsuitable. Bad language and fighting are two of her pet hates, and she may come very close to losing her temper if a child is being treated unfairly. However, at other times she can be very indulgent. She just loves giving pleasure and seeing contented little faces, and may forget her principles for a while, for the sake of this. She dislikes displays of emotion and tantrums, but she will do her utmost to talk her children out of 'the miseries' if they are upset. She isn't an especially cuddly person, but as her child grows up, Libra mum can be a real 'mate'. She likes to have a house full of friends and is capable of throwing the most wonderful children's parties, complete with treasure hunts, conjurors and quizzes – often she will seem to be enjoying it all more than the children!

It is very important for this mum to have a life of her own. The desire for the 'better things of life' can be so strong with Libra that she may insist that her children live out some of her 'unlived' life, encouraging intellectual and artistic talent and ignoring pleas for such interests as sport or cookery. She can't believe that anyone would turn their backs on culture and is sure that if her children miss their chance, as she did, that they will regret it all their lives. She is wonderful when it comes to encouraging most abilities but may be deaf to unspoken emotional pleas. However, catch her at the right time, when she isn't being harassed by grim realities like peeling potatoes, and she will usually listen, if her children put their case clearly. It is important to her to give everyone a fair hearing.

Libra mum loves to go to the school to discuss her child's progress. She is usually a fair parent, not blind to the faults of her little darling, and so she rarely gives teachers a hard time. However, woe betide the teacher who really *has* treated her child unfairly, or neglected him or her, for she will move heaven and headteachers to ensure that justice is seen to be done. Ms Libra will be mortified if it is her child who has written rude words all over the lavatory or come bottom of the class – she just can't understand *why* kids have to behave like that, or how she could have given birth to a dunce. However, she will do her best to ensure extra-curricular tuition is available to any of her children who need it. As her child grows Libra mother will find something to boast about, proudly exalting the achievements of her offspring, adorning the mundane or squalid with genteel euphemism or 'poetic licence'.

Libra mum is great when the children are teenagers, and she is often the confidante of the friends of her sons and daughters, discussing their problems about sex, drugs or whatever, offering them a glass of wine and a box of tissues, and generally making them feel adult. In this way she brings out the best in people. In the end Libra is much more comfortable as a friend than a parent. Probably she will turn out to be the best friend her children ever have.

■ LIBRA FATHER

Hormones ensure that Libra mother is emotionally prepared for parenthood, but Libra dad has to manage without. Fatherhood is rarely a Libran dream, and he may have observed the rowdy disorder in other households with deep misgivings. Usually all preconceived ideas dissolve as soon as the precious pink bundle is put in his arms, and if his detachment survives that, it will not last long beyond the first dimpled smile or lisped word. In the event, Libra father copes admirably, from the time of sticky fingers and screams to mudfights and pet grass snakes. There is something about his calm manner, his interest and his gentleness than can turn a little monster into a cherub. However, he does have his limits, and if pushed beyond them can lose his temper, which is something for which he will never forgive himself. This could make him withdraw, and become inaccessible to his children, which is a shame.

Libra dad can be stern on occasion. Often he expects high standards of his children. He can be very intolerant of fights and displays of spite and envy. However, mostly he is an indulgent playmate, and will come home with special gifts for his children. It doesn't take much to bring out his extravagance, and children are a brilliant excuse. Libra father is always prepared to explain his decisions to a child, and he has a way of getting through to even the smallest. Because of this he often obtains co-operation. Children, like adults, tend to respond in the manner they are treated, and because Libra dad behaves as if everyone is reasonable, usually the children are.

It will help if Libra dad has somewhere to retreat to when it all gets too discordant for him. Libra mum needs this too, of course. Libra parents need plenty of evenings out and contact with other adults when things other than children are the subject of discussion.

Libra isn't slow to spot that one advantage of parenthood is that it limits the possibility of loneliness, and Libra dad will certainly ensure that he is a friend to his children. However, it is very important to Libra that children do not destroy romance, and Mr Libra will be anxious to maintain the same relationship with his wife that he had before they became parents. He is unlikely to call her 'Mum'. It is also extremely important that the harmony of the household is not destroyed by the children or Libra father will make an excuse to escape.

Libra father is adept at pointing out the skills and accomplishments of his offspring and he will enthusiastically pin up the picture of the *Starship Enterprise* (that you would never have recognised, if it hadn't been labelled) on the notice board along with the evening class schedule. However, Libra father's need for a little peace and refinement must be catered for somewhere in each day. If this need is met, Libra dad makes a better parent, and is able to transfer an appreciation of art and beauty to the children.

■ THE LIBRA CHILD

There is a myth that Libra children are all dimpled darlings – it isn't true! However, like all myths, there is here a kernel of truth and Libra's first recourse is always to the charm. If a smile won't work, it's time for other tactics.

Little Libra responds to the domestic climate: if everyone is shouting he or she will add voice to the mayhem; if you are doing the dusting Libra must have duster *and* polish, too. Should you be provoked into hitting this stubborn cherub, Libra will hit you back. After all, fair's fair. This has a way of putting you face to face with your own reprehensible conduct and giving you some hard choices. Now you can rely on *force majeure* and smack the child into submission, which is unthinkable, or you can admit to yourself that even that little tap was an unforgivable show of violence and your child is learning primarily by example – which is more true of Libra than many children. Best to say 'Let's calm down, it's time for lunch – or a walk, or a look at a book' – anything that will restore an even tempo. Libra will always respond to consideration and sharing, but if thwarted, well . . . this is the sign of war.

We have learnt that Libra struggles with decisions, and so young Libra will benefit from being given choices as soon as possible. Keep this as simple as you can. Too many alternatives are bewildering to any child. Always keep the choices to two – an apple or an orange, Thomas the Tank Engine or Dumbo. Libra children enjoy having the power to make decisions and use their minds (but it's remarkable how often they do manage to have both, in the end!).

All Libra children discover the power of charm well before they are out of nappies. Even if they do not have the typical Venusian good looks – and many do – they still exploit their natural gifts. The old-fashioned beliefs about spoiling children have thankfully been superseded, and it will do Libra children nothing but good to have their sweet smiles and shaky handing-round of the cakes rewarded by thanks and attention. However, that Libran indulgence and laziness can appear at an early age, so don't let yourself be wheedled out of sensible habits – at heart Libra appreciates a balanced life most of all.

Discordant surroundings will affect Libra even in the nursery and every aspect of the surroundings should be chosen with care. Usually Libra responds exceptionally well to music, and if you sing to young Libra you may find those legs stop kicking and you can get the nappy on. This is usually a friendly, open child, quick to approach other children, and Libra may experience a few knocks when he or she finds that not everyone wants to share. As Libra gets older it is important that this child realises that not everyone is fair, pleasant or even safe. Like the other Air signs, friendliness may be plentiful and instinct about human nature a little thin. Be prepared to explain to Libra children at length how and why some people are dangerous to children, because they won't be fobbed off by half-truths, and it is important that they take you seriously.

Libra is often a neat sign, even when young. Yes, they will still play with their food, but they may go and get the cloth to wipe up the spillages. Grit your teeth when the milk drips on the floor for Libra will soon get the hang of it, and you'll have cause to be grateful. Vanity can be appealed to from an early age and 'Clean your teeth, so they look all nice' will get you a much better response than a simple command. Like any child, Libra will have fun grinding biscuit crumbs into the carpet, but he or she will draw your attention to it, and help you get out the vacuum cleaner – one of their first words may be 'Ugh'.

Usually Libra children are eager to learn, and it is evident that they are thinking in reasoned fashion, even before they can talk. When schooltime comes, Libra children will benefit from a well-ordered classroom environment. They may respond in kind, hollering with all the others but they will be secretly upset. This is the sign of companionship and balance and a Libran child acquires a happy glow when Mummy and Daddy are both there, and being nice to each other – and to Libra. Divorce is frequent these days and, naturally, Libra children have to adapt like all others. They will be reassured if they see that matters are being discussed in a civilised manner, and it is always a good idea to include them in family decisions.

Romance may be well in evidence long before the teenage years, for Libra needs to try out relationship skills as early as possible. Invite boys and girls to birthday parties. As adolescence approaches, get in extra mirrors – or build on an additional bathroom, if you can – you'll need it! Libra can spend more time in front of the mirror than any other. You will need to be prepared for many ups and downs, for Libra adolescents will live and die through their relationships. However, you can usually appeal to their reason and that sense of balance, as long as you listen to them. Libra teenagers can be logical, and it will make sense to them if you explain why their studies are also important, although they will have trouble actually living by that. Never lay down the law – Libra adolescents will think this is unfair and it will seem that their point of view is not important to you, so they may treat yours in the same way. Always arrive at decisions by negotiation, and polish up your wits for your Libra offspring will have intelligent arguments to support their wishes.

Libra is an accommodating sign. Libra children cannot be bludgeoned, but they can be cajoled and they will be very good at cajoling you. However, parents of Libra children must be careful here. Libran blandishments should not be over-rewarded, or Libra children may come to believe that charm gets them anything, which may be almost true, but isn't completely, and there's no substitute for hard work and self-development. In addition, it is very important that the Libran thirst for approval isn't exploited. Libra children should not be persuaded away from a career as a musician, when that is their first talent, by being told they are wonderful at Maths, their second subject, and being encouraged to take a Maths degree 'like Uncle Frank' when that may lead to a life of unfulfilment. As Libra parents must be careful not to 'live' through their children, so Libra children must not live anyone else's ideas of how life should be.

■ LIBRA AS SIBLINGS

Less extravert or captivating children may resent the attention Libra receives, and this should be noticed by adults. However, Libra is usually keen not to give offence, and a younger brother or sister with Libra strong in the chart, usually manages to wheedle the best out of the older ones. 'Goody-goody' may be hissed under the breath of a resentful sibling, as Libra gets praised *again*. However, not all Libra children are angels, as we know. Young Libra may be the very bane, arguing with the older ones. Older Libra may be impatient and critical of younger siblings, but will usually try to maintain an atmosphere of calm. However, Libras in a family react to undercurrents, and while they may be unaware of what they are doing, they may stir up discord if they sense that much is being repressed. It is better to have things out in the open. Older Libras (and even the little ones) will often stand up in defence of brothers and sisters if they are being unfairly treated by parents. No Libra will stand by and listen if nonsense is being talked, nor will they take kindly to someone else taking all the attention – again, it isn't fair. Libra siblings may take unkindly to having their individuality encroached upon by a claustrophobic family, and they may decide that families are 'uncivilised'. In time a Libra sibling can be your best friend, a partner in debate and someone to have a giggle with at family reunions. Brother or sister, mother or father, perhaps being a 'friend' is what Libra likes best of all.

■ LIBRA IN THE HOME

Libras will adapt to almost any type of dwelling, large or small, as long as it does not offend their sense of the aesthetic. These are often musical or artistic people and priority may have to be given to piano or easel. If cupboard space is lacking, make sure that things at least 'look good'. For instance, scarves hung on a hook can look lovely, if drawers are packed. Pastels and delicate designs may be favoured. It is often a help to have a handy phrase to glamourise difficult surroundings – poky can become 'charmingly bijou', or Libra may take pride in some fine original paintings to take attention away from the fact that the rest of the house is – well – scruffy. Parallels can be drawn for younger Libras, and room should be found for whatever they find lovely, even if it's a canvas of 'magic' dots that reveals a dinosaur when you look at it cross-eyed. Let Libras choose curtains and bedcovers, where possible and always accord the same respect for their space as you wish them to give you. Libra children may not be as keen to have a room of their own as some other signs, but as they get older they will need to be able to withdraw from an intimacy that they may find distasteful. It is more important for Libra that they are shown respect for their wishes and things of beauty around them than any amount of space or cupboard capacity. However, many Libras do hate mess – more so than Virgo, who is famed for it – and Libra may be drawn into helping the entire household achieve a greater standard of attractiveness.

■ PRACTICE AND CHANGE ■

- Libra parents must have regular time away from the children, and other family members will be doing a great service if they babysit.

- No Libra parent should ever have an unalleviated diet of childcare. Like all the Air signs they have a constant need for adult company.

- No one likes discord in the house, but Libra will hate a disturbed atmosphere more than most. It is best if everything is discussed openly, and Libra involved.

- You must always have the opportunity to entertain friends at home in a way you feel does you credit.

- The Libran tendency to live through or for others needs to be watched. Libra parents must be aware of their own unfulfilled aspirations and find opportunities to make them real in their own lives, not those of their children.

- All children learn by example, but none more so than Libra. This should always be borne in mind when bringing up a Libra child.

- Libra parents need to be aware of a tendency to be a little detached or to distance themselves from what is unpleasant, coarse or discordant – in short, such things as most children produce, most days. The beautiful and the eternal are reached *through* our humanity, not *despite it*, and if they are prepared to notice this, children can be a living proof.

- Listening and personal attention are deeply important to Libras, more than most. Time should be devoted in each day when family members can open out and talk, in an atmosphere of welcome and acceptance.

4 Friendships and the single life

*'It isn't much fun for One, but Two
Can stick together' says Pooh, says he,
'That's how, it is' says Pooh*

A. A. Milne

Naturally, friendships are important to all of us, whether we are married or single. However, those who are not currently in a committed relationship often find they have more time to pursue friendships and more scope to make plans with friends. Although partnerships are pivotal in the life of Libra, friends are always dear to Libran hearts. Most Libras know the true meaning of 'being a friend'.

■ LIBRA AS A FRIEND

Because Libras are so often charming, one might think that you ought to be liked by all, but this isn't always the case. Some people mistrust the Libran talent for compromise and feel you are insincere. It is unfortunate that humans generally seem to regard an ingredient of aggression as laudable and do not value the exquisite skill of keeping the peace. Libra is by no means an untruthful sign, but you will be economical with the truth – that is *not* a euphemism for lying: it is an accurate description. You will try your best to say only that which will bring pleasure; you will choose your words with care.

You will usually make your friends feel good, and that is worth a great deal. Libra is the artist of the verbal fig leaf. A friend's ramshackle garden becomes 'a romantic tangle', her messy house 'bohemian' – suddenly what seemed like a drab existence takes on a little glamour and she starts to relax.

As a friend you can be a great asset at parties, steering the topic away from controversy and topping up glasses. You are usually there for friends at life's crises, managing to be witty without being insensitive, listening to their sob story for just the right length of time, and bringing out the whisky bottle on cue. You don't like too much in the way of storms, and the whisky will emerge much earlier if your friends are hysterical. However, your patience can be exemplary. Occasionally, some Libras do pitch into the judgmental, or find themselves saying 'What did you expect', 'I told you so', and other verbal slammers that are too often aimed at those laid low. Libra may do this in the hope that next time they will 'keep their balance'. Very occasionally Libras may put their principles before friendships, however, such is a rarity. Yes, in the final analysis, Libran commitment to justice is stronger than the commitment to peace, but 'justice' to most Libras isn't far from 'kindness and consideration'.

■ LIBRA AND THE SINGLE LIFE

I am sure that I do not have to repeat – Libra doesn't *like* the single life. Being solitary simply makes you feel incomplete, and this fact has rushed many a Libra into an unwise partnership. However, if you are a Libra and you find yourself single, you do owe it to yourself to find some things to enjoy about your current status simply to prevent yourself from rushing off and making a disastrous liaison.

There *are* benefits to being single for Libra. One of them is that you can cut your toenails and floss your teeth without these intimate grooming tasks being encroached upon, or even guessed at, by anyone else. In addition, you will never encounter anyone else's dental floss or nail parings, and that may be worth a great deal! You can play your own music and hang your own pictures without any philistine opposition, and you can read in bed as late as you like. Make the best of this time. Catch up on Tolstoy, Sartre and Shakespeare – become a real 'culture vulture'. Or if something lighter is your style, enjoy the time you have with your friends. Be careful that you don't become unrealistic about life, lost in a fantasy about perfect partners and genteel living. Be careful also that you do not overindulge in alcohol or those delicious Belgian chocolates. You will need your wits and your waistline when someone new comes into your life.

If Libra can find someone congenial to share flat or house, that can be a great solution, as long as washing-up rotas and such like are sorted out well in advance. You will become physically ill if the atmosphere is discordant or the surroundings offensive, so don't take risks. Friends of Libras need to be aware that while you may seek their company, and often be very charming about it, you may not be telling them the whole truth about how you feel. Libra is not good at facing up to emotional realities and you won't like to lose your cool in front of them. 'I'm a bit solitary at times,' may mean 'I'm lonely as hell' and 'I've got one or two things on my mind,' may mean 'I'm worried sick'. You do need to open out and to trust that friends will be able to cope with your feelings even if you can't. A trouble shared is a trouble halved – and this is the sign of sharing.

■ PRACTICE AND CHANGE ■

- If you are a Libra do remember that not everyone shares your standards. You may have to be careful about being a little 'snobbish'. Ask yourself what it is you are avoiding? No one can debase you or take away your pleasure in company or the finer things of life.

- You need to remind yourself that friends are often gratified by being needed and what seems to you a frightening emotion may be easy for your friend to handle – especially if they are a Water sign.

- Some people may misunderstand your horror of aggression. Face the fact that you can't please all of the people all of the time, and some people don't *want* to be pleased.

- Extending from the above 'You can't win 'em all'. Whatever you do someone somewhere is going, at some time, to be angry and disapproving of you. Try not to worry about this.

- You are one of the signs that can take to dating agencies and singles groups, so be prepared to give it a whirl.

- You know how you love to have time to spend on improving/enjoying yourself. If you have to be single then set out to enjoy this. It may seem forced at first, but sooner or later you may catch yourself out really enjoying it.

- House or flat sharing may be a good idea but do select companions *very* carefully. Always give yourself time to think and discuss with friends, and do not let your wish to be pleasant rush you into agreeing to share with someone who is going to be messy or discordant, for few things could be worse.

5

♎︎
Career

A moral, sensible and well-bred man
Will not affront me, and no other can

William Cowper, Conversation, 193

Libra's need for grace and harmony is naturally evident in your working life. Libra has been called 'lazy' and indeed sometimes this does appear to be the case. You believe in balance in all things. All work and no play makes Jack a very unbalanced boy, and you will usually take regular breaks, or even cat-naps. Many Libras display a leisurely manner, even when they are busy and harassed, and they may lounge and loiter as if they had all the time in the world.

However, this is a Cardinal sign, geared to action, and the resting times are interludes between forays, during which you may be weighing up the next move. The relaxed Libran air is often superficial. Like the swan you may be all visible poise and composure, but paddling like mad underneath.

This equable sign is usually ambitious and while you rarely do anything as undignified as to claw your way to the top, you tend to advance on the basis of – you've guessed it – charm. This isn't by any means an oily ingratiation. Libra adapts wit and style to the surroundings, enjoying pleasing and enjoying succeeding. Not just pretty faces, Libras usually have quick and logical minds.

■ TRADITIONAL LIBRA CAREERS

The common denominator for all occupations suitable for Libras is that they satisfy, to some degree, the Libran love of balance, fairness and beauty. Libran careers include:

- diplomat
- counsellor (especially marriage counsellor)
- beautician
- dress designer
- interior designer
- hairdresser
- welfare worker
- receptionist
- valuer
- work involving physical balance (i.e. dancing, juggling)
- show business
- hospital work
- publishing
- politics
- the judiciary
- any luxury business

■ WHAT TO LOOK FOR IN YOUR WORK

The majority of people work in large insurance corporations, sales offices, shops, banks and factories. Relatively few of us can choose a profession, train for it and find a fulfilling lifestyle, and as time progresses this is becoming more elusive.

To help you find a job that suits you, you need to bear in mind the spirit of what is recommended, not the specific occupation. One office job is not like another, one job selling fashions may differ enormously from one down the street in terms of environment and opportunity. As a Libra you need to make sure of several things when seeking employment:

- Your surroundings are pleasant and aesthetically pleasing, in whatever way you define this. Colour, decor, works of art, canteen facilities – all these will contribute to your feeling, or otherwise, of well-being, and anything squalid will quite possibly affect your health. It will certainly affect your performance, so don't talk yourself out of it, if you feel uneasy. Some Libras like to work outdoors, and will find congenial surroundings that way.

● You will not have to deal with discord among your associates. This is less important if your subordinates are involved, for you will have the ability to sort that out.

● Your mind is stimulated, and the need for a little enterprise called for.

● You are reasonably sure of being treated fairly. You will chafe under injustice, not because you are a rebel but because you simply can't stand it, for yourself or anyone else.

● You will not be called upon to graft ceaselessly, or frowned upon for having a laugh and a chat at regular intervals. You achieve your best when you can be relaxed.

● In some way your talent for beautifying, harmonising, judging or balancing is called for.

● You are not going to have to work completely alone for long periods.

So there is no need to feel that you have to look for a specifically Libran job. Many Libras would feel suffocated in the judiciary or find the idea of being a performer of any sort ludicrous. Look for something that suits in its content and atmosphere, rather than its label. Don't try to make the best of a bad job – if it doesn't suit, move on.

■ 'YES-SIR-NO-SIR-THREE-BAGS-FULL-SIR'

Most Libras are anything but sycophantic, but there are those who take the charm a little to far. On flashes the 200-watt smile every time the boss walks in. 'Three-bags-full-Sir' will open doors and offer chairs so unfailingly he or she seems to be on a spring. These people always seem to be witty and au fait, even the day after the office party, when everyone else has mouths that feel like the bottom of birdcages and matchsticks propping open their eyes. Three-bags-full never argues or whines.

Three-bags-full is usually sincere in seeing the best in everyone. What is lacking in them is the ability to see anything good in themselves. These are likely to be people whose appearance is almost faultless and whose mind is not slow (it can't be, to think up all that convoluted verbal candyfloss). These people don't feel like anybody unless they can see themselves in the smiling eyes of someone else – preferably someone in authority – and gain that delicious look of approval. Perhaps the kindest thing that can be done for Three-bags-full is to get them out where they can be induced, by fair means or foul (but not *too* foul, this is a Libra, after all) to let their hair down and let the real person out, who may be truly entertaining. Three-bags-full needs to realise that compliments don't buy inner fulfilment, or popularity with peers.

■ THE ARISTOCRAT

If given half a chance the 'Aristocrat' will talk about articles read in *Tatler* or *Vogue,* and about exotic holiday destinations. Aristocrats will pepper their speech with the odd French phrase. Aristocrats may make colleagues feel inferior; alternatively, Aristocrats may make colleagues laugh – usually they are quite easy to see through – and others may tease them – just a little.

The Aristocrat is rather a sad Libra figure, so patience is needed. Here we have a socialite/designer/foreign ambassador manque, and it is probably true that Aristocrat has talents that have never been exploited. Aristocrat has probably been forced, at some point in life, to cope with conditions that were quite appalling, offensive and demeaning, and the only way of coping with it is to magnify anything gracious in life and embellish it with a little fantasy. Make a note that *you* will leave no stone unturned in life to avoid such a condition. And if you recognise yourself here, isn't it time you found a way to get real? Join the debating/operatic/literary society.

■ THE LIBRA BOSS

This boss is usually 'one of the guys (or girls)', popular and approachable. Often exceptionally well groomed, this person chooses the office decor with care. Employees should remember *never* to leave empty crisp packets on their desks or dirty macs over the backs of chairs, and avoid being vulgar in this person's hearing, until they have found out the threshold. Libras *can* be coarse and profane but they have a way of doing it with style, so employees need to make sure they know which style and whether they can match it.

In all probability the Libra boss will notice the good jobs employees do and compliment them, their appearance and the cup of tea they made this morning. The boss may ask employees' opinions on everything from the colour of the office carpet to the company merger, and employees shouldn't feel too crestfallen when their carefully considered opinion – which was listened to, so attentively – is disregarded, or when they overhear their boss asking the cleaner and the caretaker for their views also. This is all part of the Libran process of weighing things up. Libras value the opinions of others on the way to making up their own minds, and employees' opinions will have been valuable as part of this. This Libra did not get where he or she is by being foolish.

In small matters Libra may drive others mad by not deciding, but should not have decisions made for them. Suggestions, yes – decisions no, or employees will have far more trouble on their hands. They will need to be patient as they sit with phone or notepad in hand waiting for instructions, and even more patient when Libra changes her or his mind and they have to phone the customer back and make apologies – but then, they must be good at the blandishments by now, for they have the finest teacher!

This boss tries to be fair in all respects and will usually meet employees halfway. However, if they expect too much they'll get nothing, for Libran justice will decree that they get back what they give. This person is definitely not a pushover – go too far and employees will be politely but ruthlessly put in their place – and that might well be out of the door. It is essential never to argue or be vindictive in front of Libra, but to be always as judicious and affable as the boss – it's a valuable talent to learn.

■ THE LIBRA EMPLOYEE

These people must have pleasant surroundings. They shouldn't be stuck at a scruffy desk, looking at the damp patches on the wall, if the boss wants to get the best out of them, and should always be treated fairly and honestly. Libras can be quite militant about worker's rights, and their views about this and other issues should be listened to, for usually they will have logical merit. Employers should ask the views of their Libra employees about anything and everything – often they will have a creative solution, and even if they don't they will probably have something to say that throws new light on the matter, or at least makes them feel that things aren't so bad after all, and there is a way of managing the situation.

If a Libra employee is caught picking a sneaky chocolate from their desk drawer, flirting in the corridor or simply staring out of the window, it is best to turn a blind eye. The boss didn't employ a child of Venus to have them drudge and beaver, he or she hired them – or should have done – for their talents. Libra just can't work non-stop, but that doesn't mean employers aren't getting their money's worth, because Libra will make up for lost time – after all, fair's fair. Libra will greatly help the atmosphere in many offices, encouraging open debate – and sometimes surprisingly astringently – and then calming things down. Some Libras can act as good mediators between management and workers, because of their ability to see all sides, and yet they do not like to work in a bad atmosphere. They will make efforts to improve this. Employers shouldn't distrust their charm – make it work instead. These days it is too prevalent to assume that assertiveness and aggression are the right and proper means to achieve anything. Libra has other, and better methods.

■ WHEN UNEMPLOYMENT STRIKES

Most people are frightened at the prospect of loss of income and Libra is no exception. However, typically, people of this sign do not panic about this. I knew a Libra man, who, having found his journey to work terribly unpleasant, just didn't turn up the next day. Lo and behold he was offered a post in a branch near his home! There is a limit to what Libra will endure in order to stay in work, and many Libras relish time off to pursue hobbies – often Libra will have a hobby that is almost as important as work. It's that penchant for 'balancing' again.

If Libras feel they have been sacked or made redundant unfairly they will feel very hurt and will seek recompense ruthlessly. This isn't someone you get rid of without due consideration, so any employer taken in by the co-operative manner – beware. Some

Libras are truly afraid of losing their jobs, because of the loss of quality of life, and these may become quite jittery if this happens. Now Libras may do their two-headed giraffe act, not knowing which way to turn and arguing themselves out of every alternative.

If this should happen to you, remind yourself of your assets. You know how you can get on the right side of people, turning most situations to your advantage. Hopefully, you also have a healthy respect for your mental abilities. Of course, you will feel undecided, but you do not have to make any decisions. Now is the time to explore as many alternatives as possible. Keep as many irons in the fire as you can and add to them, daily. Spend plenty of time with friends and try not to minimise your distress. No one will find it offensive that you are sleepless with worry, nor will they step in and control you on the basis of it. Of course, cultural pursuits, expensive nights out and foreign holidays will have to go on the back burner for a while, but it is only a matter of time before you find a new job and the balance is restored once more.

■ SELF-EMPLOYMENT AND OTHER MATTERS

Not all work relies on a company and an employer, for there are many other approaches. You are very resourceful and often talented. You can be extremely creative especially where human relationships are concerned, and some traditional Libran talents – for example, design – lend themselves to freelancing. It is very appealing to Libra to have the freedom of freelancing, and often you do very well, for there is a natural appreciation of ebb and flow in the sign. You are quite capable of self-motivation and of structuring life so that all gets accomplished and there is time for recreation. Two drawbacks present themselves, however. You are rarely happy alone for extended periods and budgeting is definitely not your forte. Safeguards for this need to be set in place, if possible.

■ PRACTICE AND CHANGE ■

- You must have pleasant working conditions. This mean the surroundings themselves should be pleasing and there should be the minimum of discordance from and between other employees. Failing this, you may be unable to work and may be ill.

- You need to work at your own pace. This may seem slow, but probably it isn't in the least, in fact the opposite may be the case – Libra often has a leisurely air. You need to take breaks as and when you feel the need, in order for you to give of your best.

- Just because you can seem like airheads – bubbly and inconsequential – others should never make the mistake of underestimating your intelligence. Usually it is very sharp and needs to be used in your work.

- Fairness is a keyword for Libra, and must always be born out in every facet of your working life.

- Loneliness at work should be avoided. If you are in an office alone you may waste time by going out to look for company. Usually (but not always) you work better in a group or partnership.

- Despite the fact a Libra boss may be affable and accessible, he or she is anything but a pushover. Libra bosses shouldn't be pushed too far – their spines are solid steel.

- Libra employees often make excellent mediators, and will often help the atmosphere simply by their presence. This Libran talent deserves to be exploited.

6 Healthy, wealthy – and wise?

I want . . . to be at peace with myself . . . to live . . . an inner harmony, essentially spiritual, which can be translated into outward harmony

Anne M Lindbergh

■ HEALTH

Astrological reflections on health, even when based on the entire birth chart, may be of doubtful value, because health is such a complex issue. What may we usefully say about the health of Libra in general?

Libra is ruled by Venus, planet of love and harmony. Venus, however, is also related to pleasure. Pleasure is a wonderful thing, as we all know, and it is certainly a gift of the goddess. However, it is possible to have too much of a good thing, and you can occasionally lose your sense of balance in respect of the good things of life. So chocolates, cakes and other delicious food can be a temptation to excess which you need to avoid, or there can be a possibility of overweight, or other complaints. However, some Libras do go to the other extreme and adopt the ascetic approach, possibly in the belief that it is more celestial. Ideally, Libra needs to enjoy goodies in moderation. You may also be tempted into drinking too much alcohol, or possibly smoking or other inadvisable habits. Here the self-indulgence of Libra manifests, and not in a balanced way at all. If you recognise this in yourself, you need to retrieve your sense of harmony in health as in all things.

Of great importance to Libran health is the harmony of your surroundings. You can be incapacitated, or even made ill by garish or squalid circumstances, and you, with characteristic tact, may find it very difficult to complain. Nor are you likely to be taken seriously by less sensitive people – you have the intelligence to be aware of this and it will add to the problem. Of equal importance is the emotional climate and many Libras can become distressed if there is an atmosphere of discord. Up to a certain point you will happily play peacemaker, but if this doesn't work you may feel very jittery, and this will inevitably take its toll on the immune system and the body generally.

Suppressed negative feelings may also be detrimental to Libra – a trait you share with the other Air signs. You do not like to admit discordant emotions into consciousness. Anger, grief, jealousy, hatred – all these are natural human reactions to certain types of situations, but you may prefer to 'rise above' them or simply deny they exist. However, this does not make them go away, and they may emerge as phobias, anxiety or depression, which are more difficult to deal with. You need to use your excellent mental powers to understand and accept these factors, not to reason them away.

Kidneys and lower back

Libra is said to rule the kidneys, and the association is no surprise, for the kidneys keep the 'balance' in the components of the blood. Libran overindulgence may result in too much stress on the kidneys, leading to lassitude and possibly to skin troubles, which you will find most distressing. Another balancing factor is, of course, the back and many people (certainly not just Libras) do suffer from back trouble. Our upright posture is what distinguishes us from other animals, but it is also responsible for many of our chronic back problems. All the Air signs treasure the dignity of humanity, but back pain can be a metaphor for the possible distress caused by neglect of our animal nature. Of course, it is also the result of poor posture, movement and the strains and stresses of everyday life.

Libra can occasionally be a little 'stiff' in approach, being refined and idealistic. A stiff back is a reminder to 'loosen up' and employ some of that Libran grace in dance, walking or movement. You are always so careful of your appearance and you should cultivate balanced posture and graceful movement, which will bring much pleasure and enhance health. In addition, you must be careful to take regular breaks when working, for periods of unremitting graft will make you ill. A classic symptom of overwork is back pain, caused by too much lifting, or sitting too long at a desk.

You may find oriental therapies such as acupuncture and Chinese herbalism of value in restoring balance to the body and to the immune system. While you may recoil from invasive methods, the gentle healing arts may appeal to this sign.

■ MONEY

It has to be said that Libra is not usually 'good' with money. Despite your best intentions you are seldom proof against the appeal of the delicate '*je ne sais quoi*', the elegant artefact, silk scarves and ties and all manner of adornment and accoutrement that is lovely, but rarely useful (or even a sound investment). You Libras also like to buy little presents for your friends and much money can trickle away in coffee bars, restaurants and pubs, spent on refreshments and companionship.

Often, however, it does seem that this sign has a 'guardian angel' when it comes to money, for just when the bailiffs appear on the horizon, a benefactor arrives with a timely handout, or you receive a legacy, tax rebate or share bonus that was quite unexpected. Libran charm extends to a 'charmed life' where money is concerned – usually, that is.

This is not to say that Libra does not worry about money. This sign does not have the devil-may-care optimism of Sagittarius or quite the Leonine conviction that they are children of the gods (aristocracy, yes, gods, no) Often Libras will be found wringing their hands with worry because they have overspent *again*, but these are resourceful people, and a solution can usually be found.

There are, indeed, some Libras who are very uptight about money, hating the thought of the indignity of impoverishment, and these will be very controlled about the pennies, but they are in the minority. Hyacinths for the soul are a Libran priority – and sometimes it seems they grow into a money tree.

■ WISDOM

It will be no surprise that Libran wisdom centres upon balance and harmony – two crucial Libran motifs. A Libra who is at peace with herself, or himself, will be a centre of harmony for all around. 'All things in moderation, nothing to excess' are the Libran mottos. Some Libras are drawn to the Chinese wisdom of the I Ching, the Middle Way, and understand that 'the way that can be told is not the constant way, the name that can be named is not the constant name'. Such Libras also understand the native American concept of 'walking your talk' so that life is an expression of harmony and wisdom. It may take Libra a while to achieve inner peace, but it is the goal of all Libras, and most know the value of cultivating it.

■ PRACTICE AND CHANGE ■

Health

● You need to remind yourself to express your feelings more, in the interests of health. Where expression is unsuitable or inadvisable, you should at least make the effort to *recognise* how you feel, for allowing the feeling into consciousness is 90 per cent of the battle.

● Moderation is attractive to you in theory, but you may need to make more effort to put it into practice. Too often you are drawn into excesses of self-indulgence, and when tempted you need to remind yourself of your overall priority.

● Harmonious surroundings are a 'must'. Do not put up with the discordant in any form. It isn't worth it, for the sake of your well-being.

● Remember the importance of posture and movement in respect of health and balance. The way we hold ourselves has many implications for our well-being.

Wealth

● Like all extravagant people you may need to 'tie up' some of your salary in regular investment, to ensure that it can't be frittered away.

● If you are trying to save money, avoid scenes of temptation. Allow yourself little treats to keep you away from the big ones, or plan chats with friends or other pastimes to compensate. Be aware that your social life does not make too many inroads upon your purse.

7 ♎ Style and leisure

It is absurd to divide people into good and bad.
People and either charming or tedious.

Oscar Wilde

■ YOUR LEISURE

As a Libra you are sure to value your leisure – indeed you may set great store by it. However, if you have to spend too long doing nothing you will become restless and fidgety. Although you certainly do have periods of lethargy, these rarely last long, unless you have become depressed by the uncongenial, or by overwork. So your leisure time needs to be quality time, where you have stimulating things to do and naturally amusing company.

During your free time you may like to seek out places of natural beauty, for to you a 'thing of beauty' truly is 'a joy forever' or you may gravitate to works of art or spend a great deal of time getting lost in fine music. I once saw a play where the heroine, wafted to her door by funereal strains, exclaimed 'Wouldn't you just die for Mahler!' Such a Libran sentiment! Many Libras at some time express similar viewpoints, and whether it's Mahler or Madonna it amounts to the same thing. Painting, sculpting and screen painting might appeal, and while Libras are not always actually artistic, they are almost always devoted appreciators.

Many times we have observed that Libra likes company and this may be especially evident in leisure time. However, you do not always suffer fools gladly, and while you will be eternally polite, you choose companions with care. Wit and an entertaining personality are high on your list of priorities. It is important that interests are shared – Libra looks more for intellectual rapport than emotional support, although this can leave you somewhat high and dry at times of crisis.

This is a Cardinal sign, and so despite the love of harmony, you are often competitive and relish sports where this can be expressed. Games that can be played doubles may appeal, such as badminton or tennis, but you are not averse to face-to-face combat, because the 'rules of the game' mean that any unsightly aggression is well contained. In fact, this is generally an active sign and many activities may appeal in moderation. Eastern discipline such as T'ai Chi or certain martial arts may also be attractive for their smoothness and balance. Dancing may be especially favoured, and Libras may enjoy ballroom dancing or jive, for you are often excellent at matching your movements to that of another. Occasionally we may come across the type of Libra who is 'stiff' trying to maintain the rigid balance that we explored earlier. In this case, dance will be especially beneficial, although there may be a resistance at first. One Libra I know describes herself as the most awkward person alive (which is rare for this sign). However, once at a party she got drunk and danced the tango from start to finish without a single false move, on the table tops, with a rose between her teeth! The ability is there, although dormant.

Libras like to take rambles with friends, because it gives them the chance to walk and also to look at lovely scenery. Gardens may have similar appeal, likewise all the usual attractions such as galleries and exhibitions. Libras often like to wander around stately homes, partaking of the erstwhile elegance. In addition, Libras love any cultural pursuits, debating or literary societies and the like. Whether in search of refinement or just a good time down at the local, you know the meaning of 'pastime'.

Holidays

These are necessary to Libra – the sign produces few workaholics, and you, all things being equal, have little trouble jetting off and leaving it all behind you. Again, it is important for you to have companions, and these must be the right ones. This sign is not typically attracted to solitary excursions, and planning it all with a friend is half the fun. It has to be said that the toffee-nosed aspect of Libra can come out in respect of holidays, and you will love to be able to drop the names of exotic locations into your after-dinner chatter. You love to have a holiday that 'sounds good' and will use 'poetic licence' where possible. So a trip on a grubby old boat will become a 'cruise' or if you just *have* to go to boring old Minorca you may airily refer to 'slumming it – my friend wants to go, you know'. This is all harmless and part of the fun. After all, what's life without a little glamour? No life at all, to Libra.

■ YOUR STYLE

This has all the exquisite elegance of a Chinese painting, and many Libras are specifically attracted to Oriental art. The oriental wisdom of feng shui may appeal especially to Libra, as it is based on harmonising the surroundings, and many Libras instinctively have much skill in this respect. Elegance, delicacy and accord are important – there should be nothing harsh, nothing that jars upon the senses. All should convey an ambience of serenity. Indeed, you often have the gift of being able to make very minor alterations in a room or a outfit that render the effect exquisite, when before it was ordinary. Colours for you need to be well-chosen. Often blue is favoured, or possibly shades of rose. Pastels may appeal, but also crisp contrasts, where appropriate. In clothing, you sometimes like the tailored approach, sometimes the casual, depending on what is appropriate to the occasion. Libra women often have the knack of looking extremely feminine; similarly, the men often look masculine, although with a gentle air. Libras often like to spend a great deal on their appearance, regularly frequenting the salons of beauticians and hairdressers.

Living space needs to be tasteful and airy. You usually like to have well-chosen works of art on display. You don't like to be confronted with disorder, but nor does your sign enjoy having to put lots of effort into keeping things clean and tidy. Provisions should be made so that any muddle is unobtrusive, and attention drawn to what is attractive, instead. Many Librans like to have on show something a little unusual as a conversation piece and also as a reminder that life isn't all grey Mondays.

When choosing purchases for yourself think 'harmonious, beautiful, balanced, artistic, refined, cultured, delicate, elegant, peaceful'. It will be very hard for you to resist anything you see that you find beautiful. Try not to buy on impulse. Take the time to think over whether this article will fit in with the rest of what you have. You may decide you do not want it, if it will upset the balance of what you have already acquired.

■ PRACTICE AND CHANGE ■

● Your leisure time is very important to you. Make sure that it does not just 'happen' to you. Plan activities and the people you wish to spend time with.

● Indulge your love of beauty regularly. Do not deprive yourself of attractive things upon which to feast your eyes – it will be balm to your soul.

● You need mental stimulation. Without it you may become depressed, without knowing why. Seek out people with vitality and pursuits that 'stretch' you. Seek always to improve your understanding and your level of information.

● Make room in your daily routine for some time with the artistic or the beautiful, however you define it.

● Companions are important for holidays, but if there are no suitable companions available, do not be afraid to go alone, preferably on a holiday where you are sure of meeting people. Your pleasant manners ensure that you will make friends, and these may turn out to be good ones.

● If you are at all dissatisfied with your surroundings, try to step back and take a detached, fresh view of the space. What is it that is out of balance, in poor taste or in some other way displeasing? Do not be tempted to keep something, however lovely it may be, if it does not fit in. It is important to you to have harmonious surroundings, and what is beautiful can become ugly in the wrong setting.

● Similarly with your clothes. Anything that makes you feel less than glamorous, or that is not chosen for some specific occupation should go. You will never feel good in it.

Appendix 1

◼ LIBRA COMBINED WITH MOON SIGN

Our 'birth sign' or 'star sign' refers to sign of the zodiac occupied by the Sun when we were born. This is also called our 'Sun sign' and this book is concerned with Libra as a Sun sign. However, as we saw in the Introduction, a horoscope means more than the position of the Sun alone. All the other planets have to be taken into consideration by an astrologer. Of great importance is the position of the Moon.

The Moon completes a tour of the zodiac in about twenty-eight days, changing sign every two days or so. The Moon relates to our instincts, responses, reactions, habits, comfort zone and 'where we live' emotionally – and sometimes physically. It is very important in respect of our intuitional abilities and our capacity to feel part of our environment, but because what the Moon rules is usually non-verbal and non-rational; it has been neglected. This has meant that our lives have become lop-sided. Learning to be friends with our instincts can lead to greater well-being and wholeness.

Consult the table on page 81 to find which sign the Moon was in, at the time of your birth. This, combined with your Sun sign is a valuable clue to deeper understanding.

Libra Sun / Libra Moon

You are a dynamic peacemaker and you love to create the beautiful or begin projects of a creative nature. Probably you love company,

Find your Moon number

Look up your month and day of birth. Then read across to find your
personal Moon number. Now go to Chart 2, below.

January		February		March		April		May		June	
1,2	1	1,2	3	1,2	3	1,2	5	1,2	6	1,2	8
3,4	2	3,4	4	3,4	4	3,4	6	3,4	7	3,4	9
5,6	3	5,6	5	5,6	5	5,6	7	5,6	8	5,6,7	10
7,8	4	7,8	6	7,8	6	7,8	8	7,8	9	8,9	11
9,10	5	9,10,11	7	9,10	7	9,10,11	9	9,10	10	10,11,12	12
11,12	6	12,13	8	11,12	8	12,13	10	11,12,13	11	13,14	1
13,14	7	14,15	9	13,14	9	14,15,16	11	14,15,16	12	15,16,17	2
15,16,17	8	16,17,18	10	15,16,17	10	17,18	12	17,18	1	18,19	3
18,19	9	19,20	11	18,19	11	19,20,21	1	19,20	2	20,21	4
20,21	10	21,22,23	12	20,21,22	12	22,23	2	21,22,23	3	22,23	5
22,23,24	11	24,25	1	23,24,25	1	24,25	3	24,25	4	24,25	6
25,26	12	26,27,28	2	26,27	2	26,27,28	4	26,27	5	26,27	7
27,28,29	1	29	3	28,29	3	29,30	5	28,29	6	28,29,30	8
30,31	2			30,31	4			30,31	7		

July		August		September		October		November		December	
1,2	9	1	10	1,2	12	1,2	1	1,2,3	3	1,2	4
3,4	10	2,3	11	3,4	1	3,4	2	4,5	4	3,4	5
5,6,7	11	4,5,6	12	5,6,7	2	5,6	3	6,7	5	5,6	6
8,9	12	7,8	1	8,9	3	7,8,9	4	8,9	6	7,8	7
10,11,12	1	9,10	2	10,11	4	10,11	5	10,11	7	10,11	8
13,14	2	11,12,13	3	12,13	5	12,13	6	12,13	8	12,13	9
15,16	3	14,15	4	14,15	6	14,15	7	14,15	9	14,15	10
17,18	4	16,17	5	16,17	7	16,17	8	16,17,18	10	16,17	11
19,20	5	18,19	6	18,19	8	18,19	9	19,20	11	18,19,20	12
21,22,23	6	20,21	7	20,21,22	9	20,21	10	21,22,23	12	21,22	1
24,25	7	22,23	8	23,24	10	22,23,24	11	24,25	1	23,24,25	2
26,27	8	24,25	9	25,26,27	11	25,26	12	26,27,28	2	26,27	3
28,29	9	26,27,28	10	28,29	12	27,28,29	1	29,30	3	28,29	4
30,31	10	29,30	11	30	1	30,31	2			30,31	5
		31	12								

Find your Moon sign

Find your year of birth. Then read across to the column of your Moon number.
Where they intersect shows your Moon sign.

Birth year					Moon number											
					1	2	3	4	5	6	7	8	9	10	11	12
1900	1919	1938	1957	1976												
1901	1920	1939	1958	1977												
1902	1921	1940	1959	1978												
1903	1922	1941	1960	1979												
1904	1923	1942	1961	1980												
1905	1924	1943	1962	1981												
1906	1925	1944	1963	1982												
1907	1926	1945	1964	1983												
1908	1927	1946	1965	1984												
1909	1928	1947	1966	1985												
1910	1929	1948	1967	1986												
1911	1930	1949	1968	1987												
1912	1931	1950	1969	1988												
1913	1932	1951	1970	1989												
1914	1933	1952	1971	1990												
1915	1934	1953	1972	1991												
1916	1935	1954	1973	1992												
1917	1936	1955	1974	1993												
1918	1937	1956	1975	1994												

(The body of this chart is a grid of zodiac symbols.)

Ari	Tau	Gem	Can	Leo	Vir	Lib	Sco	Sag	Cap	Aqu	Pis

also, but you may find other people quite a distraction when it comes to making up your mind. It is hard for you to know how you really feel at the best of times, because you try to feel how you think you ought to – peaceful, tolerant and fair. When the wishes of others have to be taken into account you usually acquiesce to these and may find yourself in compromising situations. You do need co-operative relationships, but your emotional equilibrium truly depends on a truthful relationship with yourself, first and foremost. Give yourself the peace and seclusion to discover what you really feel. You may decide then to let that take a back seat at certain times, but at least you will have been honest with yourself.

Libra Sun / Scorpio Moon

You have great dynamism with which to infuse your creative projects. The trouble is you sometimes shoot yourself in the foot by being too intense or emotional. Despite the fact you despise feelings such as suspicion, jealousy and vengefulness, and although you value the honourable, somehow you get sidetracked into the manipulative and you cannot help some dark, brooding thoughts at times. Your castles in the air have some fearful dungeons! You owe it to yourself to bring your inner feelings up into the light of day. Allow yourself to experience a whole range of feelings, not just sexual ones. Infuse your relationships, your peacemaking efforts and your social activities with real passion, rather than fiercely controlling yourself and presenting a bland face.

Libra Sun / Sagittarius Moon

Your talent for looking on the bright side makes Polyanna look like a misery guts. You know there is a moral in everything if you can only find it, and you are dynamic when it comes to cheering everybody up, making jokes and infusing all with optimism. You are a great philosopher, in every sense of the word, and you are interested in the meaning of life and in having a good time. Sometimes you procrastinate and you can avoid important issues by making light of them or focussing on the spiritual of the futuristic when what needs to be grappled with is the 'here and now'. Sometimes you need to stop being such a ray of sunshine or rolling stone and stay and face both your own true feelings and those of others, not to mention the rough necessities of life. Nurture a true sense of the spiritual to give you the toughness to face reality.

Libra Sun / Capricorn Moon

You continually frustrate yourself, for while you wish to appear gregarious and warm there is a reserve within you, making you hold back. You may find yourself alone and frustrated. It is important to you to do the right thing, and you may be eternally seeking standards and approval instead of developing your own inner yardsticks. Probably you are a stern perfectionist and you may have little tolerance for your own, or others' deviance from what you identify as the straight and narrow – and yet you may feel very unsure and insecure at times. You may feel you can be loved only if you are 'perfect' but that is not the case. Learn to meet your inner needs by creating structures of beauty and balance that satisfy *you*, not anyone else. You have immense talent for solid and aesthetic achievement, and you can 'build peace'.

Libra Sun / Aquarius Moon

You are a true idealist, friendly to all with cherished beliefs about how people should behave and relate to each other. You are humanitarian in a personal and a general way, and you will always hold out your hand to help – but rarely for help, for you fear not to be self-sufficient. Probably you have many friends because you have the gift of charm and understanding, but no one ever gets very close, and you can become unpredictable when pushed. Freedom is vital to you, and you would defend the right of anyone to hold their opinion, even if you do not agree with it. However, one 'freedom' you may not be championing is that of yourself to feel what you truly feel, not what is 'nice'. Choose friends who will validate your uniqueness and who will enable you to open out emotionally and use your mind to understand yourself, not to reason away what is not 'civilised'.

Libra Sun/Pisces Moon

You are one of the most sympathetic souls alive and you will do a great deal to create harmony and peace and to console anyone who is upset. You are the supreme idealist. Your dreams are not of perfection in people or society but of a world where all is warmth, love, caring and romance. Life itself may often appear unkind, uncouth and brutal to you, but all the same you do not lose your faith. You have the gift of compassion, so much so that you may lose yourself in other people, and indeed your ideal may be to achieve just that experience of oneness. However, to lose yourself in a way that means bliss rather than dissolution means that you need first to find yourself. Open your heart first to your own pain and need, as well as joy. In this way your encounters and endeavours will have greater depth.

Libra Sun/Aries Moon

There is a demanding side to your nature that sits uneasily with your wish for harmony and balance. Just when you think you are being your most tactful, out slips a remark that goes down like a lead balloon. You can't help trying to be one up when equality is the keynote, and impatience and frankness strain against urbanity and diplomacy so that you feel pulled apart by horses. Actually you are a very intuitive person and are able to achieve a great deal in terms of interpersonal relationships and all enterprises simply because you are aware of the personal and the collective, and you have an inner dynamism as well as a wish for peace. You are able to see both sides of anything with a clarity that may be uncomfortable but is potentially very creative. Take note of your dreams – occasionally they may be prophetic – and look inwards to the vibrant core of your being rather than always outwards for validation and stimulation.

Libra Sun/Taurus Moon

The aesthetic and the sensual meet in you, creating a potential either for the artistic or the self-indulgent. You appreciate fine foods, fine wines and gratifying sex. Sometimes indolent, you take the line of least resistance, and when pushed you may resist passively. If you are not satisfied with life you may take refuge in overindulgence in food, alcohol or other pleasures that are not in your best interest. Your appreciation of life is rich and deep. Potentially you are very creative, but you may not value yourself and may remain caught in unproductive habit patterns. Looking to others for validation, you may seek tangible proof of your worth in attractive gifts and attention. Seek the internal balance that assesses and satisfies your true needs and identifies your deepest resources – this will make you feel healthy as opposed to 'sticky inside'. Do not feel you have to hold on so tightly – what is rightfully yours will always come to you.

Libra Sun/Gemini Moon

Probably you are an asset at any party, for you have wit and vivacity. Communication is your lifeblood and you are a party animal –

unless you just happen to be the more introverted bookworm type, in which case you may be very well informed, for your hunger for knowledge is second only to your hunger for relationships. If you are feeling dissatisfied or insecure you may have 'verbal diarrhoea' or flit, butterfly like, from one person or idea to another without finding real nourishment. It is all too possible that you may reason yourself out of your emotions, in which case you may become highly strung, ceaselessly seeking deep contact and emotional gratification but never allowing yourself to find it. Deep inside it may be too threatening to face your feelings, but you must use your keen mind to make sense and reality of your needs, not to reason them away. In this way you can achieve true intimacy and nourishing relationships.

Libra Sun / Cancer Moon

You may need people more than you are willing to admit and by accommodating them and meeting their needs you seek to achieve satisfaction. However, this can rarely be possible unless you are sharply aware of exactly what you are hoping to get, for others may simply take advantage of you. You can be a dynamic carer with a wish to 'mother' the world, but make sure you are appreciated. Do not unconsciously fall into self-pity, but use your energies to crusade for charities or conservation. You have the ability to empower your ideals with real depth and passion. Do not disparage your feelings. Use your sense of balance and fairness to allow them due place in your life.

Libra Sun / Leo Moon

You bask in affection and approval like a big cat in the sun. For you, everything needs to be glamourous and just a little larger than life. It is likely that you have 'star quality'. If you feel loved and at the centre of everyone's universe you can be the soul of generosity.

Entertaining, charming and a little theatrical, you can also become a little unrealistic or vague at times, as if you are lost in a world of your own. You have a great deal to give, as long as you can appreciate even when there is no applause. Remember when you are seeking appreciation always to look inwards, to your internal yardstick, and if you do not have one then that is something to be developed. If you find you are compulsively seeking attention, then you need to develop true self-love, as opposed to vanity. You may discover yourself through play, through giving love from the depths of your heart as well as just receiving. Find also true balance from admitting pain as well as joy, which will give you immense strength of character and resolve.

Libra Sun / Virgo Moon

You do need to be careful that you do not disappear up your own posterior through endless analysis and search for perfection. You will find yourself stuck up a dead end and everlastingly frustrated if your yearning for beauty is short-circuited by an obsession for order. When you are upset or threatened you may avoid facing this and lose yourself in compulsive work, when you should be seeking company. Learn to appreciate the rosy apple-cheeks instead of looking for the worm in every fruit. The truth of the matter is that you have an outstanding talent for aesthetic perfection and for a precision that is so exact it is breathtaking. Develop realistic standards that admit the beauty of imperfection. Do love yourself, warts and all. Then you will have more love to give, and so you will receive more and the positive circle will intensify. Remember not to analyse away your feelings, for they are your principal asset. Life is for living – walk in beauty. No one recognises it more poignantly than you.

Appendix 2

■ ZODIACAL COMPATIBILITY

To assess fully the compatibility of two people an astrologer needs to have the entire chart of each individual, and while Sun-sign factors will be noticeable there is a legion of other important points to be taken into account. Venus and Mercury are always very close to the Sun, and while these are often in the Sun sign, so intensifying its effect, they may also fall in one of the signs lying on either side of your Sun sign. So, as a 'Libra' you may have Venus and/or Mercury in Scorpio or Virgo, and this will increase your empathy with these signs. In addition the Moon and all the other planets including the Ascendant and Midheaven need to be taken into account. So if you have always been drawn to Piscean people, perhaps you have Moon or Ascendant in Pisces.

In order to give a vivid character sketch things have to be stated graphically. You should look for the dynamics at work, rather than be too literal about interpretation – for instance, you may find that you are attracted strongly to Capricorns, although you may also be aware that you are dissimilar. It is up to the two of you whether a relationship works, for it can if you are both committed. Part of that is using the awareness you have to help, not necessarily as a reason for abandoning the relationship. There are always points of compatibility, and we are here to learn from each other.

On a scale of 1 (worst) to 4 (best), here is a table to assess instantly the superficial compatibility rating between Libra and companions:

Libra 3	Aries 1
Scorpio 2	Taurus 2
Sagittarius 3	Gemini 4
Capricorn 2	Cancer 3
Aquarius 4	Leo 4
Pisces 1	Virgo 1

■ LIBRA COMPATIBILITIES

Libra with Libra

This is a mutual admiration society. Naturally you are likely to share an attitude to life and to enjoy the same things. However, it may not be easy to come to a decision, as each is too considerate and wants the other to decide. This may mean that you are all dressed up to go out, sitting on the sofa politely debating whether to go to a film, play or restaurant until well after closing time. The best way to resolve this is to take it in turns.

As lovers There is much gentleness and consideration between you. You may share a taste for erotica and may find each other surprisingly assertive between the sheets. However, you may take so long setting the scene and getting in the mood that the moment has passed when you really begin. You will like to be seen as a 'beautiful couple' – Ms Libra loves this man's good manners and Mr Libra admires this lady's exquisite taste. However, you may get quite irritated at the other's endless co-operation, detachment and unwillingness to decide, and you could bring out the worst in each other, as time goes by. You may spend too much time talking about the relationships so your encounters lack real passion. Both of you need to take the plunge and let your guard down, before you become like two parallel lines, always equidistant, never meeting up.

As friends   You may bring out the argumentative side of each other and enjoy debate. There may be a little subtle oneupmanship between you, about who is the most cultured or well informed, and you may turn up your noses in tandem at 'the plebs'. You are sure to enjoy going out together, and may compliment each other *ad nauseam*.

As business partners   Making decisions and managing money will be your dilemmas. You are both creative and skilled with the public but must not overspend on making an impression.

Libra with Scorpio

With the two of you it's *'Vive la difference!'* Libran cultured elegance sits uneasily with Scorpionic passion and intensity, and yet the two are often attracted. Libra, friendly to all and flirtatious to many, may drive Scorpio mad with jealousy, while Scorpio may depress Libra with emotional swamp trips. However, the bond between you may be strong.

As lovers   The sexual side is likely to be superb, for Scorpio adds dimension to Libran style, while Libra refines all the Scorpionic emotionalism, so that we have something that can build in the rhythm and dramatic fervour of Ravel's *Bolero* – unforgettable! Ms Libra is hypnotised by the depth of this man, while Mr Libra is drawn by the unspoken sexuality of Ms Scorpio. In the long term, Libra can become a little frightened of Scorpio, going to ludicrous lengths not to provoke a mood or scene, even when the relationship is well past its sell-by date. Scorpio is not above using emotional manipulation, and Libra creates a cool, polite distance – this can go on for far too long. However, these two have much to offer each other and this relationship deserves effort. Scorpio needs Libran balance as much as Libra needs Scorpionic emotionalism.

As friends   Without the sexual element there may be little to attract the two of you. The Scorpionic 'pressure-cooker' personal field may make Libra uneasy while Scorpio dismisses Libra as superficial. However, you may enjoy discussing aspects of relating and find you need each other in ways you hadn't imagined.

As business partners   If you are able to respect each other this can work well, for Scorpio has tenacity and money sense while Libra enjoys PR and social contact.

Libra with Sagittarius

You are likely to find each other great fun. Sagittarian indestructible good humour and bonhomie is very attractive to Libra and you may be found, shoulder to shoulder, looking on the bright side and raising your glasses as Armaggedon rolls in. Libra may find Sagittarius somewhat tactless and may get fed up with repairing the social blunders, while Sagittarius loses patience at Libran indecisiveness and trots off to do their own thing, which will be hurtful to Libra. Nonetheless, a good time can be had by all – mostly.

As lovers   Attraction may be strong at first because everything seems suffused with sunlight and optimism. It may feel as if anything is possible, and in a way it is. Ms Libra finds this man very entertaining and Mr Libra is bowled over by the independence of Ms Sagittarius, that takes the pressure off him to act macho. It may seem to others that you are a golden couple, but the gloss can wear thin after a while. Sexually Libra may find Sagittarius rather rough and unsubtle in the long run and Sagittarius may accuse Libra of being contrived. Worst of all, Saggittarius may leave Libra unexpectedly alone when the impulse takes them to some lone adventure, or off with other companions who don't take all day to make up their minds to comb their hair. Work is needed if this relationship is to be more than a good time, with little depth.

As friends There will never be a shortage of pastimes to interest the two of you. Sagittarius supplies the adventure and Libra gives it all panache. Interestingly, Sagittarius isn't much better at decisions than Libra and may dismiss details with a sweeping wave, feeding Libra's exquisite salmon sandwiches to the bird's a few hours later, saying 'I prefer cheese' – well, you could have told me!

As business partners More dash than cash, although your charm may save you. A Taurus or Capricorn may provide a safety net.

Libra with Capricorn

Libra may find Capricorn rather dour and reserved, and yet there is something about the understatement and effectuality of Capricorn that can appeal to Libra's sense of the aesthetic. Capricorn has no problem with decisions, which can be balm to Libra, who obliges by lightening the life of the Goat in tasteful ways that never fail to find favour – except when they cost too much!

As lovers A good sexual relationship is possible between you and is important for the continuance of the relationship, and for warmth. Ms Libra admires the firmness of Mr Capricorn, which she senses can give a balanced structure to life, while Mr Libra is impressed by the *savoir-faire* of Ms Capricorn. Problems can materialise when Capricorn is called upon to talk about the relationship, because concepts are not Capricorn's 'thing' – doing is far more their style. Libra does need fair words, and may nag, which makes the Goat clam up even more. Still, Capricorn is capable of an old-fashioned romanticism, which charms Libra. One area of conflict could be money, for Libra does need pretty bits and pieces, while all Capricorn is interested in is usefulness and budget.

As friends   Libra can soften the life of Capricorn and gently introduce them to interests beyond the utilitarian. Capricorn adds structure and decision, which can make Libra feel they are achieving something. However, Libra will not take to being 'managed'. Libran rationality is appealing to Capricorn, who may well try out new pastimes on that basis.

As business partners   We know that Libra likes to create a good impression. Capricorn, on the other hand, is more concerned with substance. Capricorn should hold the purse strings, but not too tightly.

Libra with Aquarius

Two Air signs make an excellent combination. Aquarius has loads of ideas and is often avant-garde – this fascinates Libra, and the two of you could talk for hours. Both of you like to be seen as pleasant and civilised and you are each extremely idealistic, with a different emphasis, for Libra is the more personal, Aquarius social. Aquarius may turn out to be too detached for Libra to achieve the quality of relationship desired.

As lovers   You may be quite sexually inventive at the start. Ms Libra admires the breadth of ideas and intellectual gymnastics of which Mr Aquarius is capable and some of his crazy ideas leave her speechless. Mr Libra adores this individualistic woman. Aquarius may be too stubborn at times for even Libran tolerance. On the plus side, Aquarius is happy to discuss the relationship, but Libra may be irritated by the Aquarian's habit of linking it all to the current political climate or comparing it with man/woman interaction in ancient Japan.

Ideally, Libra wishes for more intimacy than Aquarius can manage, and the sex life may cool until the relationship is merely platonic, which will never keep Libra happy.

As friends You share so much in your attitude to life and there are sure to be interests in common. You may work together for social reform, attend talks together or just talk. This can be a beautiful friendship.

As business partners Aquarius may not appreciate the need to make a good impression as much as Libra does – Aquarius expects people to look at the essence. Libra should handle interpersonal relationships, for Aquarius may be too dogmatic or eccentric, when it comes to the point. Some Aquarians are good with money – if not, you will need assistance from elsewhere.

Libra with Pisces

There can be a blissful, dreamy quality to this relationship. Pisces can be just as tactful as Libra and much more intuitive about knowing what people want to hear. The main problem here could be decisions, for both want the pleasure of knowing the other is pleased. Libra may end up having to decide, doing it after the bus has gone, and both end up disgruntled.

As lovers Air and Water are often very passionate together, and this relationship can have a vivid fantasy element. Ms Libra feels that at last she has met a really sensitive man, while Mr Libra feels protective towards Ms Pisces, and deeply appreciated. Piscean emotionalism, because it is gentle, often appeals greatly to Libra, who thinks they can mould Pisces into the image of perfection, like Pygmalion. They can't. Pisces slides away into a world that Libra cannot enter while Libra relentlessly weighs all the Piscean dreams and finds them wanting. These are two such idealistic people that they should be able to get on wonderfully, and indeed they can. However, because their dreams are rarely the same they may disappoint each other unless the relationship is worked at.

As friends You can both lose yourselves in the beautiful and if your tastes coincide you will find it very gratifying to go out together. You may both have the feeling that the other really knows how to enhance life. The problem may eternally be where to go, and when, and how . . . ?

As business partners This is not a good match, and unless one or both of you has plenty of planets in Earth signs, financial disaster is likely. However, you both bear charmed lives, and if the enterprise is creative and imaginative, it could work . . . .

Libra with Aries

Here the sign of relationships meets the sign of 'me first'. Aries may distrust Libran tact and call it evasiveness. 'Say what you think!' storms Aries. Libra can turn quite argumentative and obstructive, purposely prevaricating because they resent being pushed, even if they do not want to decide, either. However, these zodiacal opposites have much to offer each other, for Aries may learn that concern for others can sometimes be the most effective way to get what one wants, while Libra may appreciate that life is simpler when one goes for what one wants, honestly and openly.

As lovers Aries responds to the romantic atmosphere generated by Libra, for it appeals to their imagination, while Arien ardour, as long as it doesn't go too far, can satisfy Libra's need for everything to be put into the relationship. There are few half measures with Aries, and Libra may be thrown 'off balance'. The emotional tension this creates can be a dynamic attractant or a repellent – it depends how aware the couple are. Ms Libra certainly feels bowled over by this man's decisiveness and warmth, while Mr Libra admires Ms Aries verve and independence. Not easy, but potentially very fulfilling.

As friends You may share ideals and you will get on better if there is a cause or interest that unites you. Intimate tête-à-têtes are likely to result in tension, with Aries sniping and Libra taking up a position of superior intelligence and detachment.

As business partners Libra always needs a partner who is sensible with money and it is rarely Aries' role to provide this. If financial restraint can be brought in from elsewhere, if Aries has room for boundless initiative and Libra handles relationships of all kinds, this can go far.

Libra with Taurus

Two Venus-ruled signs, and you both love beauty and comfort. Taurean enjoyment is very sensual, however, while Libra is aesthetic and refined. After initially believing that much is shared Libra may find Taurus coarse and slow, while Taurus wonders whatever Libra is going on about. Taurus is not good at talking about the theory of anything, let alone relationships, which, after all, are about sex and practicality. To that Libra has one response – ugh!

As lovers Sex can be deeply fulfilling, with Taurus adding depth and stability to the romance of Libra. Both are turned on by ambience, scent, fabric and Taurus will not notice that for Libra most is happening in the head, or Libra that Taurus is functioning from the neck downwards. Ms Libra loves this man's seductive masterfulness and his appreciation of the beautiful, while Mr Libra thinks this is the sexiest lady he has ever encountered. If Taurus can learn a little subtlety and Libra to keep their feet on the ground, this can work. Libran flirts need to beware Taurean possessiveness, and each must have their share of expensive goodies. This could be a relationship where love goes out through the window when the wolf comes in through the door.

As friends   You may share a love of art or music. If your tastes coincide much pleasure can be found in galleries, gardens, concerts and the like. Taurean pragmatism deals effortlessly with Libran hesitation, at the best of times.

As business partners   A potentially excellent duo. Both of you are creative, Taurus is practical with money and Libra is a charmer.

Libra with Gemini

Second only to two Geminis, the pair of you can talk the hind legs off a donkey. Gemini may want to change the subject before Libra feels that everything has been discussed, especially when the relationship is the focus. Life may be a social whirl as friends come in through the front door and back door and chat through the window. All of this may distract you from the fact there isn't all that much depth to the relationship.

As lovers   This can be fine, although sexual coolness may develop sooner rather than later. Gemini might not mind this much, but it won't fit in with Libran ideas of love. Libra is the more romantic and Gemini may upset Libra by being unpredictable, impatient or just not there when Libra wants company. Ms Libra is strongly attracted to this witty, urbane individual, while Mr Libra is galvanised by this vivacious lady. Mostly this relationship is light and bright, and neither of you may notice that there is a certain something – a mystery, a wonderment – missing. On the other hand, if you *do* notice, what fun it would be finding it!

As friends   There can be no better partnership, for Libra finds Gemini stimulating and Gemini admires the polish and panache of Libra. You are likely to share ideas and intellectual rapport, and will greatly enjoy entertainment together, or perhaps going to classes, lectures and debates.

As business partners   Here there are lots of ideas but no one may want to get their hands dirty. Libra can be indolent and Gemini can prevaricate. Despite all the talk, nothing may get off the starting blocks. If it does, it could be excellent if it involves personnel, training or anything involving people.

Libra with Cancer

Both of these signs enshrine relationship, but Libra is much more cerebral about the entire matter and may frustrate Cancerian need for closeness, without having a clue what is going wrong. Neither sign likes to be alone, although Cancer may feel alone even when Libra is there and Libra may feel suffocated. For this to work Cancer needs to be prepared to talk and Libra to expose their true feelings.

As lovers   The sensuality of this duo may be poignant and delicate. It may be hard to get started because you are backward in coming forward, Libra through endlessly weighing pros and cons, and Cancer through fear of being hurt. Libran tact may circumvent Cancerian sensitivity for a while, but Cancer may still be wounded by Libran detachment and this will try Libran patience. Ms Libra delights in the sensitivity of this man, while Mr Libra responds to the femininity of gently caring Ms Cancer. You have much to offer each other and can be a good complement, but you must work at it.

As friends This can be an enduring and caring friendship. Libra will support Cancer with companionship and a little sensitive wit, while Cancer can show Libra that it is safe, and quite civilised, to express one's deepest needs and gain solace.

As business partners This can be good, for you are creative together. Cancerian imagination and Libran style make a unique combination that can be appealing, sensitive and relevant. In your different ways you each have an instinct for what people want. Cancer is good at smelling out rats and watching the money while Libra usually has more salesmanship.

Libra with Leo

At first this can work very well indeed, although Leo's high-handed attitude may wear away Libran tolerance. Libra will gracefully take half the blame but will balk at an unalleviated diet of humble pie. Leo could just be a little jealous of Venusian charm and wonder if he or she is the only sun in the Libran sky, and it will take all Libra's tact to cope with this. You may have lots of social functions, but intimacy could be a little thin.

As lovers Leo's commitment answers some of Libra's requirements regarding partnership. Ms Libra admires the dramatic and confident Leo persona which is generally stylish, while Mr Libra is pleased to have this goddess on his arm. In time, Leo may be a little too intense for Libra, while Leo may become fed up with Libra accommodating everyone else, and not always available to pay due attention to the Lion. Sex may be very good at the start, and you each appreciate romance. However, there is a difference in emphasis which may become evident after a while. Leo is less of an idealist and wants both to be consumed by the relationship. Besides, to Leo, the relationship is there to enhance their ego, at least in part. Libra, however, gets off on the partnership ideal, which Leo may violate. Neither of you has much idea about emotional bonding, but this may not matter.

As friends Together you can light up the town, if you wish. Any functions planned by you have a good chance of combining flair and presentation. However – who does the washing-up?

As business partners The sky's the limit – at least as far as the debts go! To be fair, you each have panache, vision and talent, but someone, somewhere is going to have to call a halt to expenditure, at least until you have made your first million!

Libra with Virgo

This is an interesting combination, because in some ways you have much in common. Libra is the real perfectionist of the zodiac, although Virgo usually walks off with the laurels in this respect. Actually, Virgo is a realist. If Virgoan practicality can be directed to lay foundations for Libran castles in the air, then things may work well, but if Virgo is hell-bent on finding the dry rot then ruin will result.

As lovers For refinement and technique you two are unparalleled. Ms Libra respects this man's reserve and discrimination, and Mr Libra finds Ms Virgo's restrained sensuality irresistible. Libra will resent too much in the way of criticism, and in true 'fair's fair' style may insist on repaying in kind, ever so subtley. Continual niggles may be destructive and you may irritate each other, Virgo by pecking away at everything with pragmatism and Libra by waxing lyrical, to compensate. Virgo may become frustrated if life becomes one round of social activity. Extremes of passion and emotion may be lacking, but neither of you may mind, and with your excellent taste and talents for discrimination, this relationship can work well, as long as you meet each other halfway.

As friends Libra may come to rely on Virgoan skill to help with plans, valuing their opinions on many subjects, for Libra trusts that Virgo will notice things that might offend Libra at a later date. Virgo can relax a little with Libra, enjoying life in the assurance that all is in the best possible taste.

As business partners This can work, as Virgo may be content to keep everything rolling behind the scenes, while Libra has lots of schemes and charisma. Libra may find Virgoan thriftiness galling, but it is an asset, as long as it does not become too much of a choke-lead.

Appendix 3

■ TRADITIONAL ASSOCIATIONS AND TOTEM

Each sign of the zodiac is said to have an affinity with certain colours, plants, stones and other substances. Of course, we cannot be definite about this, for not only do sources vary regarding specific correspondences – we also have the rest of the astrological chart to bear in mind. Some people also believe that the whole concept of such associations is invalid. However, there certainly do seem to be some links between the character of each of the signs and the properties of certain substances. It is up to you to experiment, and to see what works for you.

Anything that traditionally links with Libra is liable to intensify Libran traits. So if you wish for some reason to be incisive and provocative, you should steer clear of the colour soft blue and rose and ylang-ylang essential oils! However, if you want to be your harmonious Libran best, it may help to surround yourself with the right stimuli, especially on a down day. Here are some suggestions:

- **Colours** Shades of mid to pale blue, turquoise, shades of rose and pink.
- **Flowers** Rose, apple blossom, lilac, magnolia, orchid, sweet pea, violet.
- **Metal** Copper, lodestone.
- **Stones** Lapis lazuli, turquoise, chrysoprase (i.e. apple green chalcedony).

Aromatherapy

Aromatherapy uses the healing power of essential oils both to prevent ill health and to maintain good health. Specific oils can sometimes be used to treat specific ailments. Essential oils are concentrated and powerful substances and should be treated with respect. Buy from a reputable source. *Do not use any oil in pregnancy,* until you have checked with a reputable source that it is OK (see 'Further Reading'). *Do not ingest oils* – they act through the subtle medium of smell, and are absorbed in massage. *Do not place undiluted on the skin.* For massage: Dilute in a carrier oil, such as sweet almond or grapeseed, two drops of oil to one teaspoon of carrier. Use in an oil burner, six to ten drops at a time, to fragrance your living area.

Essential oils

- **Rosewood** Balances the nerves and dispels the inclination to daydream. It is doubtful whether the use of this oil is ethical, as huge amounts of trees have been chopped down, in the Amazonian rainforests. Ho-wood oil is a substitute.

- **Thyme** This oil is a strong antiseptic especially of the respiratory organs. It is good for relieving asthma and helps resist infection. Bracing and healing for muscular aches and pains, or rheumatism.

- **Ylang-ylang** A voluptuous and dreamy oil, also linked to Pisces. It regulates the heart rate and respiration and is useful to treat trauma. It can also help with sexual dysfunction and to heal jealousy and resentment.

- **Rose** This beautiful oil is also very gentle. It relaxes and soothes all intense emotions, helping gynaecological problems and post-natal depression.

Naturally you are not restricted to oils ruled by your sign, for in many cases treatment by other oils will be beneficial, and you should consult a reputable source for advice if you have a particular problem. If a problem persists, consult your GP.

▌ YOUR BIRTH TOTEM

According to the tradition of certain native North American tribes, each of the signs of the zodiac is known by a totem animal. The idea of the totem animal is useful, for animals are powerful, living symbols and they can do much to put us in touch with our potentials. Knowing your totem animal is different from knowing your sign, for your sign is used to define and describe you – as we have been doing in this book – whereas your totem shows you a path of potential learning and growth.

The totem for Libra is the Crow, and you also have affinity with Grizzly Bear and Butterfly. You were born in the Falling Leaves Time. There is a difficulty here, for North America lore is based on the seasonal cycle. For those of you in the Southern Hemisphere, it may be worth bearing in mind the totems for your opposite sign, Aries. These are Falcon, also Eagle and possibly Hawk, although Hawk is for the Fire clan. The Aries time is called Awakening Time.

Crows are scavengers, and while this may not appeal to aesthetic Libra, scavenging is a useful function and encourages balance in nature and full use of resources. Crow can link Libras to their opportunist and resourceful attributes. There are many varieties, including magpie, and you may have heard the rhyme 'One for sorrow, two for joy . . . ,' etc. in regard to magpies, which is interesting, considering Libra's dislike of loneliness! These are gregarious birds, at home on earth or in the sky. Their habit of looking at the world first through one eye and then the other makes it appear they are seeing both sides. Symbolically, Crow is a law-giver and a protector of secrets, bringing knowledge of cosmic law.

Contacting your totem

You can use visualisation techniques to make contact with the energies of your birth totem. You will need to be very quiet, still and relaxed. Make sure you won't be disturbed. Have a picture of your totem before you, and perhaps burn one of the oils we have mentioned, in an oil burner, to intensify the atmosphere. When you are ready, close your eyes and imagine that you are your totem animal – imagine how it feels, what it sees, smells, hears. What are its feelings, instincts and abilities? Keep this up for as long as you are comfortable, then come back to everyday awareness. Write down your experiences and eat or drink something to ground you. This can be a wonderfully refreshing and mind-clearing exercise, and you may find it inspiring. Naturally, if you feel you have other totem animals – creatures with which you have an affinity – you are welcome to visualise these. Look for your totems in the wild – there may be a message for you.

Further reading and resources

Astrology for Lovers, Liz Greene, Unwin, 1986. The title may be misleading, for this is a serious, yet entertaining and wickedly accurate account of the signs. A table is included to help you find your Rising Sign. This book is highly recommended.

Teach Yourself Astrology, Jeff Mayo and Christine Ramsdale, Hodder & Stoughton, 1996. A classic textbook for both beginner and practising astrologer, giving a fresh insight to birth charts through a unique system of personality interpretation.

Love Signs for Beginners, Kristyna Arcarti, Hodder & Stoughton, 1995. A practical introduction to the astrology of romantic relationships, explaining the different roles played by each of the planets and focussing particularly on the position of the Moon at the time of birth.

Star Signs for Beginners, Kristyna Arcarti, Hodder & Stoughton, 1993. An analysis of each of the star signs – a handy, quick reference.

The Moon and You for Beginners, Teresa Moorey, Hodder & Stoughton, 1996. Discover how the phase of the Moon when you were born affects your personality. This book looks at the nine lunar types – how they live, love, work and play, and provides simple tables to enable you to find out your birth phase and which type you are.

The New Compleat Astrologer, Derek and Julia Parker, Mitchell Beazley, 1984. This is a complete introduction to astrology with instructions on chart calculation and planetary tables, as well as clear and interesting descriptions of planets and signs. Including history and reviewing present-day astrology, this is an extensive work, in glossy, hardback form, with colour illustrations.

The Knot of Time: Astrology and the Female Experience, Lindsay River and Sally Gillespie. For personal growth, from a gently feminine perspective, this book has much wisdom.

The Astrology of Self-discovery, Tracy Marks, CRCS Publications, 1985. This book is especially useful for Moon signs.

The Astrologer's Handbook, Francis Sakoian and Louis Acker, Penguin, 1984. This book explains chart calculation and takes the reader through the meanings of signs and planets, with extensive interpretations of planets in signs and houses. In addition, all the major aspects between planets and angles are interpreted individually. A very useful work.

Aromatherapy for Pregnancy and Childbirth, Margaret Fawcett RGN, RM, LLSA, Element, 1993.

The Aromatherapy Handbook, Daniel Ryman, C W Daniel, 1990.

Useful addresses

The Faculty of Astrological Studies
The claim of the Faculty to provide the 'finest and most comprehensive astrological tuition in the world' is well founded. Correspondence courses of a high calibre are offered, leading to the internationally recognised diploma. Evening classes, seminars and summer schools are taught, catering for the complete beginner to the most experienced astrologer. A list of trained consultants can be supplied on request, if you wish for a chart interpretation. For further details telephone (UK code) 0171 700 3556 (24-hour answering service); or fax 0171 700 6479. Alternatively, you can write, with SAE, to: Ref. T. Moorey, FAS., BM7470, London WC1N 3XX, UK.

Educational

California Institute of Integral Studies, 765 Ashbury St, San Francisco, CA 94117. Tel: (415) 753-6100

Kepler College of Astrological Arts and Sciences, 4518 University Way, NE, Suite 213, Seattle, WA 98105. Tel: (206) 633-4907

Robin Armstrong School of Astrology, Box 5265, Station 'A', Toronto, Ontario, M5W 1N5, Canada. Tel: (416) 923-7827

Vancouver Astrology School, Astraea Astrology, Suite 412, 2150 W Broadway, Vancouver, V6K 4L9, Canada. Tel: (604) 536-3880

The Southern Cross Academy of Astrology, PO Box 781147, Sandton, SA 2146 (South Africa) Tel: 11-468-1157; Fax: 11-468-1522

Periodicals

American Astrology Magazine, PO Box 140713, Staten Island, NY 10314-0713. e-mail: am.astrology@genie.gies,com

The Journal of the Seasons, PO Box 5266, Wellesley St, Auckland 1, New Zealand. Tel/fax: (0)9-410-8416

The Federation of Australian Astrologers Bulletin, PO Box 159, Stepney, SA 5069. Tel/fax: 8-331-3057

Aspects, PO Box 2968, Rivonia, SA 2128, (South Africa) Tel: 11-864-1436

Realta, The Journal of the Irish Astrological Association, 4 Quay Street, Galway, Ireland. Available from IAA, 193, Lwr Rathmines Rd, Dublin 6, Ireland.

Astrological Association, 396 Caledonian Road, London, N1 1DN. Tel: (UK code) 0171 700 3746; Fax: 0171 700 6479. Bi-monthly journal issued.